FROST FAIRS
TO FUNFAIRS
A HISTORY OF THE ENGLISH FAIR

ALLAN FORD AND NICK CORBLE

AMBERLEY

Dedicated to those show people who have been such a great inspiration over the years: Tommy Messham, Ron Taylor, Wally Shufflebottom and Betty Allen.

First published 2017

Amberley Publishing
The Hill, Stroud,
Gloucestershire, GL5 4EP

www.amberley-books.com

ISBN: 978 1 4456 6152 0 (print)
ISBN: 978 1 4456 6153 7 (ebook)

British Library Cataloguing in Publication Data.
A catalogue record for this book is available from the British Library.

Typeset in 10pt on 13pt Celeste.
Typesetting by Amberley Publishing.
Printed in the UK.

Contents

G. E. Dixon's Fair comes to town in the early 1900s, with its Galloping Horses, Cokernut Shies and Musical Orchestraphone!

Introduction

The twinkling of coloured lights, a cacophony of familiar tunes punctuated by screams, a cocktail of smells from hot dogs, candy floss and popcorn, mingled with diesel fumes, the tingle of anticipation – it can only mean one thing: the fair has come to town! As you get nearer the lights get brighter, the music gets louder and the all-pervading atmosphere draws you in like a moth to a flame. Your senses take over and you are drawn into the moment. As you move closer, it's difficult to imagine that the thrill you are feeling is one that has been shared by others, on this same patch of ground at the same time of year, quite possibly for centuries.

People have come together to share experiences since time immemorial – it is part of the human condition. Where large crowds have gathered, and where money has changed hands, so too have there been other people willing to entertain them and help them part with that money. In this book we look at the evolution of the funfair in Britain, starting 2,000 years ago but focusing on more modern times, looking at the history of the funfair and considering in more detail some of the elements that make the funfair the attraction it remains today, as well as how these are rooted in deeper traditions.

What is the essence of the funfair that makes it so enduring as part of our national consciousness? What does the funfair say about us as people and our need for diversion from our daily lives? Who are the people prepared to travel the country to entertain us and what are their stories? What might the future hold in store? All these questions are tackled in these pages, so roll up, roll up... let's get the show started!

The Authors

Allan J. Ford is active in a number of fairground-related areas. He started working for Tommy Messham's Wall of Death in the 1960s and travelled his own Wall of Death show under the Motordrome Co. name during the 1980s to 1990s, as well as a small walk-round Freak Show. He still rides his Indian motorcycle on the Wall when he gets the chance. These days he spends his time travelling the country, cataloguing and photographing the showman's way of life. Allan is currently chairman of The Amusement Catering Equipment Society and is on the Board of the Amusement Device Inspection Procedures Scheme, which regulates the annual testing of all the fairground equipment in the UK by a team of highly qualified engineers. In conjunction with Nick, he has written on the Wall of Death, as well as the canals – another subject close to his heart. He is much in demand as a public speaker on these subjects, and on fairground history, and can be contacted at indianscoutrider@hotmail.com.

Nick Corble has written over twenty books, usually focusing on an aspect of our heritage and how it still reflects how we live today. Additionally, he is a regular contributor to magazines and newspapers, both national and regional. Nick is perhaps best known for his writing on the canal system and the Wall of Death, often in collaboration with Allan. Nick's output has also covered fiction, via walking and football. Further details of all his work can be found on his website www.nickcorble.co.uk, where he can also be contacted. Nick is also active on Twitter as @NickCorble and on Facebook as Nick Corble (Writer).

If you enjoy this book, you may also enjoy *A History of Fairground Transport* (Amberley, 2016) by the same authors:

1

The Customs of the Realm

One of the marks of civilisation is the desire for people to come together, to gather and share and to be part of each other's lives. In the past, such occasions may have been sparked by a need to worship together, or to celebrate a saint's day, or may have been driven by wanting to share a significant moment in the agricultural or astrological calendar, such as spring fertility rites, the autumn harvest or a summer solstice. More prosaically, there would almost certainly have been practical reasons, such as to trade or exchange scarce resources. Such gatherings offered opportunities, both for those who had travelled to be there, and those who saw a crowd in terms of its potential to make money, and it is in such gatherings that the origins of the fair can be traced.

Expressions of this human need can be traced right back to ancient times, with the Romans bringing their desire for order by instituting *nundinae*, or markets, which were held every ninth day. These events means that those living in the rural hinterlands could not only trade, but also hear Roman laws being proclaimed. During these markets booths, tents and wooden stands would be erected in the forum, offering attractions and distractions beyond purely functional needs.

In the UK, records exist of Roman fairs and markets at Helston in Cornwall, Barnwell in Newcastle and St Giles Hill in Winchester, where the Tin Way from Cornwall met the Gold Way from Wales, as well as along Hadrian's Wall. These markets were accompanied by a court known as the *venalium et forum judiciale*, where disputes were arbitrated and justice was performed. The Romans were also responsible for giving us the word 'fair', which is based upon the Latin word '*feria*', meaning holy day, which became our word holiday, and was used to describe festivals or gatherings outside regular markets that were usually dedicated to a Roman god.

The human compulsion to gather continued after the Romans left, albeit in a diminished form, becoming highly localised in nature and largely driven by pagan rituals. The Viking invasions from the eighth century onwards brought disruption to the southern half of the island, but the Norman Conquest saw a return to relative stability, and over the following two centuries the number of established fairs grew rapidly.

This period was accompanied by two other trends that helped fuel this expansion. The first of these was the rise in the power of the established Church – a phenomenon that was

Market weights and measures at a
Roman market.

encouraged by the Crown as part of the process of establishing order through the feudal
system. This was accompanied by a frenzy of church-building, which of course needed
funds, as did the general process of what would today be called nation-building.

The second trend was significant population growth, and rising prosperity within that
population. It has been estimated that between 1100 and 1300, the population of England
rose from 2.25 million to 6 million, and that the proportion living in towns doubled to
around 20 per cent, with London booming in particular. People were also becoming freer
(before the Conquest, a significant proportion of the population were effectively slaves),
as well as richer, with self-employment growing and an increasing specialisation of
labour emerging.

This growing economic activity led to a greater need for trade, and early on William
the Conqueror passed a law that forbade 'any market or fair to be held or suffered except
in cities of our realm and in the walled boroughs and in castles and in the safest places,
where the customs of our realm and our common right, and dues of our crown, which were
constituted by our good predecessors, cannot suffer loss or fraud, nor violation; for we will
that all things be done with right forms and openly, and in accordance with judgement and
with justice'. In effect, the Crown had asserted a royal prerogative, or monopoly, on trade
through markets and fairs.

This was a power that successive kings used to the benefit of both the Treasury and
the Church through the granting of royal charters. This was essentially a franchise system

under which a village, town or church (usually an abbey or priory) would be given a right to hold a fair for a specified period, with the date or feast also being defined, along with the location – all in return for a fee that was payable to the Crown, or was earmarked for a church. An early example of this was a charter granted by Henry I in 1123 to the Augustine Priory Hospital and Church of St Bartholomew in London, which was to be held on the saint's feast day (24 August).

It was the Normans' successors, the Plantagenets, who really exploited this power however. While around sixty fairs were mentioned in the Domesday Book in 1086, over 2,200 charters to hold markets and fairs were issued by English kings in the seventy years after 1200, with a further 1,600 following in the subsequent 130 years. Many of these markets centred on livestock, with cattle being driven to the place of sale in order to be slaughtered close to where they were needed, seeing as there was no way of preserving fresh meat. At this time, most of the main thoroughfares were drovers' roads, which were protected by the monarch in order to ensure the safe passage of livestock.

Geese in particular were in high demand around Christmas, and whole flocks would be driven to markets, their feet having been dipped in hot tar with sand to help them withstand the long treks involved. These markets would produce crowds, and where there were crowds, there was money.

As well as towns, markets would take place at natural confluences, such as a river crossing, with examples including Shalford in Surrey, Wallingford in Oxford, Axbridge in Somerset and Bradford on Avon in Wiltshire, which in turn became the locations for smaller markets and popular fairs. Sometimes it was more appropriate to auction cattle on common land outside a town, such as Clapham, Barnet, Ealing and Wandsworth Commons around London as well as Hampstead and Black Heath (so called because victims of

The November Sheep Fair at Stamford in the late 1800s.

the Black Death were buried there). These too became established fairs, many of which survive today.

Commerce was not the only reason to hold a fair, with other popular spots being the location of a gibbet, as nothing attracted a crowd like a good hanging, although these were also often at the crossroads of drovers' ways, such as at Combe Gibbet on Inkpen Beacon, Berkshire, or Warminster's St Laurence Fair, which is also known as the Hang Fair. Many of the fairs initiated under royal charters were new, reflecting the trends in population and growing power of the Church as noted previously, while others were granted to markets and fairs that had generated a tradition of their own in the period before the Conquest, which were known as 'prescriptive fairs'.

Under the charter system, fairs became more ordered events, at least at the legal level. For example, an Act was passed in 1328 regulating the length of time for keeping fairs, stating that 'No person shall keep a fair longer than he ought to do and that every Lord at the beginning of his fair shall then do cry and publish how long the fair shall endure, to the intent that merchants shall not be at the same fairs over the time so published, upon pain to be grievously punished towards the King'. As an example of this, a statute from Northampton issued in the same year stated that any merchant who continued trading beyond the given time would have to forfeit double the value of his goods to the king.

The official civic opening of today's charter fairs can be traced back to this Act, with the reading of a charter by the mayor, proclamations by a town crier, the ringing of bells, or even the hoisting of a leather glove to demonstrate royal patronage all regular rituals. A stone cross was erected in the middle of most towns and villages, and it was from here that dignitaries would declare the fair open, which was often followed by a church service. Near to the cross, a set of stocks and a pillory would also be erected, just in case they were needed.

Although both Henry III and his son Edward I had banned the holding of fairs in churchyards, they continued to be held there until Henry VI finally managed to stop them with the Sunday Fairs Act of 1448. At the same time it was also declared that fairs or markets should not be kept on Ascension Day, Corpus Christi, Whit Sunday, Trinity Sunday, Good Friday nor any Sunday, except the four Sundays in Harvest. It's perhaps worth noting that under this law it remained acceptable to hold a fair on Christmas Day.

Wherever large crowds gather, especially if they are off their guard and alcohol is involved, some people will be out to take advantage. Fairs may have become more ordered in terms of their legal status, but they remained attractive to forces outside of the law once under way. Pickpockets, thieves, prostitutes and rogue traders giving short measure, or selling goods not as described, were a constant problem at fairs. In an echo of the Roman system, charters therefore often included a right to hold a temporary Court of Piepowder, a name derived from the French *pied poudré,* and named after the 'dusty feet' of travellers and vagabonds.

Typically a tribunal, and often sitting in an upstairs room in a local inn, the court would dispense speedy justice, lest the miscreant upped sticks and moved on to the next fair. Punishments would often involve a fine and/or some kind of humiliation, either in the pillory, stocks, ducking stool (usually reserved for women) or being drawn in a tumbrel (a two-wheeled cart) while having to dodge rotten fruit and eggs. The last active Piepowder

Proclaiming King's Lynn Mart, 1907.

Proclaiming King's Lynn Mart, 2017.

A typical cross and stocks, Poulton-le-Fylde.

The stocks and pillory awaited those sentenced at the Piepowder Court.

The Hand and Shears was home to the St Barts Piepowder Court.

was at the Stag and Hounds public house in Bristol, and although it hadn't sat since 1870, it continued to be proclaimed in the marketplace until the court's abolition in 1971.

Sometimes events occurred that went beyond the power of the authorities to control. The Black Death, which hit Britain in 1348, was one. It has been estimated that between 30–45 per cent of the population died from the plague, which sometimes wiped out whole villages. The plague returned five more times in the second half of the century, and one of its most significant impacts was to undermine the feudal system by making labour – especially specialist labour – scarce. In 1351, the Statute of Labourers was introduced in an attempt to control wages and the supply of labour. This in turn led to the creation of a third type of fair, the 'hiring', 'statute' or 'mop' fair.

Mop fairs existed to bring labour and those needing labour together; usually on Michaelmas Day, after harvest. Typically, agricultural workers, both male and female, would gather at a certain spot in order to bargain with prospective employers, wearing a tassel on their lapel to designate a particular skill, which in time became known as a 'mop'. If an agreement was reached, this was sealed with a sum of money, known as a token, for a twelve-month contract that was subject to a one-week trial period, and the tassel was replaced with a ribbon to indicate they were hired.

Mop fairs also had 'runaway' mops a week later for those unhappy with their new employer, although they would have to return the token. This was often a problem, for in all likelihood it would have been spent at the various attractions available at the fair. A number of fairs originally associated with mops still continue today in places such as Tewkesbury, Warwick and Ashby-de-la-Zouch, and although the hiring aspect of the fair generally became less important, in some cases they retained this function right up until the Second World War.

While mop fairs proved to be of enduring value, charter fairs, with their roots in trade, began to decline in importance towards the end of the medieval period. For a time, the great fairs at places such as Boston, Stamford and Winchester attracted international status, but their importance dwindled with the rise of large, often London-based, merchants who were capable of dealing with suppliers directly. By the sixteenth century the control of trade by the Crown was being eroded by the rise of new towns lacking civic government, as well as trade increasingly being conducted through what we would regard today as shops.

The tradition of the fair was well established by then though, and people still liked to congregate and have fun together – welcoming the annual break from their often mundane day-to-day lives. Fairs enjoyed something of a revival after the Restoration and for a while were patronised by polite society, with diarist Pepys making a point of travelling to Cambridge for Stourbridge Fair and attending most of those in London. At Southwark he noted how he had seen a man eating live coals and wine glasses, as well as a horse that 'told money'.

By the early eighteenth century, theatrical booths became popular, which offered a means of sidestepping the royal licencing restrictions on permanent theatres, with both Henry Fielding and David Garrick acting as frequent performers in booths. Hand-operated roundabouts were mentioned in newspapers in the 1720s, but they were not prime attractions. As the century progressed, fairs lost their fashionable patrons and urban fairs in particular were aimed more at the emerging working classes, with an emphasis on

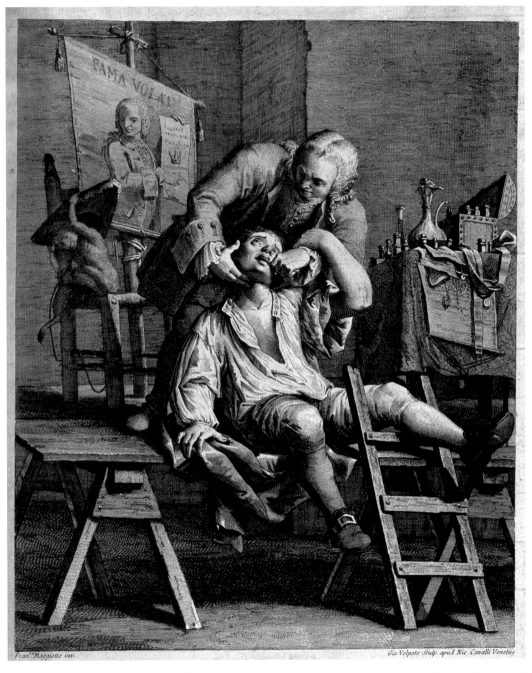

An eighteenth-century travelling dentist, as would have been common at fairgrounds around this time. (Wellcome Library, London)

All early rides would have been hand-turned.

farce and melodramas, menageries, waxworks and freak shows, as well as the ever-popular peep show.

By the dawn of the nineteenth century it was clear that wider developments such as advances in transportation through the canal network and later the railways, coupled with the growth of early factories and growing urbanisation, were bringing massive changes to society, and in their wake presenting major challenges to the showmen who ran the fairs. How they met this challenge and kept the funfair as an integral part of the nation will be covered in later chapters.

2

All the Fun of the Fair

While they may share common characteristics, no two fairs are exactly the same, and it's worth pausing to appreciate some of that variety by considering a handful of individual fairs before looking at how showmen rose to the challenge of a changing society. A history of the thousands of fairs that have taken place over the centuries would run into many volumes, and those featured below have been chosen to provide some background colour by highlighting features unusual to each before considering wider trends. A sense of the vitality of today's fair circuit can be gained from the list of current fairs given at the back of this book.

Bartholomew Fair

For centuries, Bartholomew Fair was the very epitome of the best and worst of London. As already mentioned, it dated back to 1123, with subsequent kings confirming the original charter and Edward III issuing further letters in 1364 in a charter offering the Crown's protection, partly in response to violence that had broken out the previous year. In early centuries, the fair was held inside the Priory's walls, taking advantage of the open space offered by the graveyard, as it was not regarded as sacrilegious to hold a fair there at this time. Initially, the fair was known for its plays depicting the miracles of St Bartholomew.

Many of the excesses of 'Bartlemy Fair', as it was known, were derived from the fair's proximity to Smithfield – originally known as 'Smoothfield' – where men and women were burnt at the stake during the reign of Henry IV. In 1305 the Scottish patriot William Wallace was hanged, drawn and quartered during the fair, and Wat Tyler, the leader of the Peasant's Revolt, similarly met his end there in 1381.

Smithfield was known for its cattle market, but for many years the fair offered the country's largest cloth fair, which is remembered in the names of today's Cloth Fair and Hosier Lane, with Edward III's charter actually being granted to the Draper's Company. Scattered among the fair would be numerous booths selling various sorts of small items, ranging from gingerbread and toffee apples through to mousetraps, trinkets, almanacs, hats, scarves and Bible prints. Also popular were fortune tellers, gambling dens, gin and ale tents and Punch and Judy puppet shows. Bear baiting and cockfights would add to the

The 'Fiends Frying Pan' – Bartholomew Fair in London did not have a good reputation. (The Wellcome Library, London)

scene, as would wrestling and 'musick' booths, the latter offering anything from ballads to opera. 'Freaks' resting between shows with a cup of ale could be seen, as well as prostitutes who wandered over from the popular brothels in the aptly named Cock Lane.

The fall of the sun would see tallow candles offering a half-light to watch tumblers, tightrope acts, fire eaters and sword swallowers. Following the Dissolution, the fair was owned by Sir Richard Rich, but from 1604 it came under the control of the City of London. By the end of the century the fair had grown to fourteen days and had to be curtailed back to three. Astrologers casting horoscopes and quacks selling miraculous medicines were features of the fair, while attractions such as swing-boats and the Whirligig Ferris Wheel arrived in the 1700s.

Visiting in 1815, the poet Wordsworth wrote of seeing ventriloquists and a learned pig that could tell the time. Another visitor ten years later noted an elephant that uncorked bottles and a glassblower in a glass wig blowing glass teacups for three pence. The dark side of the fair began to become overwhelming however, and the London City Mission complained to the Corporation in 1839, who eventually decided to clean up their act by closing the fair for good in 1855.

King's Lynn Mart

Starting on 14 February, King's Lynn Mart traditionally begins the fair season, running for a period of two weeks with the weather providing showmen with rain, snow, hail and a cold wind off the North Sea. King's Lynn had two marts 500 years ago and these were important trading fairs that attracted visitors from as far afield as Italy and Germany. In 1537 Henry VIII granted a charter for the Valentine Fair and it still takes place in the Tuesday Market Place, opening with an impressive ceremony preceded by a blessing on the fair and the showmen given by a chaplain. As this book will explore later, King's Lynn played a prominent part in the history of the fair as the home of Frederick Savage, a pioneer user of steam in the fairground. In 1955, the fair was honoured by a visit from their Majesties the Queen and the Queen Mother, and it continues to thrive to this day.

Mitcham Fair

Some say Mitcham Fair can trace its roots back to Elizabeth I as she was a regular visitor to Mitcham between 1591 and 1598. While this cannot be proved, we do know that attempts were made between 1770 and 1775 to stop the by-then established fair due to drunkenness, gambling and disorder. By the 1800s the fair was back on track though, with the *Morning Post* reporting a number of roundabouts, shows, booths, pony rides and refreshments. Before hamburgers and candy floss, the staple cuisine on the fairs were gingerbread, nuts,

Mitcham Fair in 1906.

toffee apples, oysters and scallops, with the latter being cheap eating at three pence for a dozen.

Initially, the fair took place in the centre of Mitcham on Upper Green, and the week before the nearby Mitcham Common would fill with large encampments of gypsies and showmen. Right up until the First World War, local children would build small grottos using oyster and scallop shells decorated with flowers that were lit with candles at the side of all the roads leading to the fair. As punters passed by the children would call, 'Throw out your mouldy coppers for the grotto.'

In 1906 the parish council tried to abolish the fair owing to traffic congestion and the imminent extension of the London Tramway, and a public protest meeting was held by the Showmen's Guild. Despite not holding an ancient charter, the fair continued to be held on Upper Green until 1923, after which Mitcham Borough Council moved it to a larger site on the Three Kings Piece, where it was opened by the mayor and town clerk in their robes and chains of office, holding a large golden key aloft to proclaim the fair open. The fair flourished in the 1950s and continued until the mid-1970s, when, like many other fairs, it succumbed to the lure of television and discos. However, in 1983, under pressure from enthusiasts and the Showmen's Guild, the council allowed the fair to return and it runs today in August.

Nottingham Goose Fair

One of the country's oldest fairs, Nottingham's Goose Fair dates back to a charter granted by Edward I in 1284, which gave status to a fair that was almost certainly already in existence marking St Matthew's Day in late September. Early on the fair was known more for its cheese than for geese, with the first reference to the fair as the Goose Fair being recorded in 1542. Geese, which were bred in Lincolnshire and driven to Nottingham, were popular for the celebration of Michaelmas, which is also around this time. Michaelmas also marked a 'quarter day', when rent became due, with tenants often presenting their landlords with a brace of geese in partial payment for their rent. Michaelmas is also often linked to an equinox in the solar calendar, marking harvest time and the end of the agricultural year.

In its early years, Nottingham's fair operated in the shadow of that run by the Priory of Lenton, whose 1164 charter forbade the holding of any other fair in Nottingham at the same time. Originally eight days long, this fair was extended to twelve days but met its nemesis with the Dissolution, allowing the Goose Fair to grow and flourish through the Tudor period, during which time it expanded to eight days.

The animal market was moved out of the marketplace in the centre of the city to ground leading up to the ash tree at the bottom of Wollaton Street in 1740, owing to overcrowding in the square and side streets. Twelve years later, the adoption of the Gregorian calendar resulted in a shift in the fair's start to early October. The fair slowly lost some of its importance and by 1800 its duration was reduced to three days. In the 1830s the entertainment element of the fair only began in the afternoon, when horse trading was complete, and as such it was not considered proper for polite society to attend until the second day.

CITY OF NOTTINGHAM

TO WIT

RUSHTON, Lord Mayor

PROCLAMATION

GOOSE FAIR, 1976

WHEREAS several Prescriptive Rights and Franchises are by divers Royal Charters and Letters Patent ratified and confirmed to the Citizens of this City amongst which a Fair is to be yearly held and kept for ever on the Feast Day of St. Matthew the Apostle, which Fair by an Order of the Secretary of State under the "Fairs Act, 1873," is to be held on the first Thursday in the month of October in each year and on two subsequent days for the buying and selling of all sorts of Cattle, Goods, Wares and Merchandizes, NOW THEREFORE the Right Worshipful the Lord Mayor doth hereby publicly notify and proclaim that the said Fair shall be here held and kept accordingly on the 7th, 8th, and 9th days of October next and doth hereby require that all Cattle, Goods, Wares and Merchandizes then brought hither to be sold shall be exposed to public view and sold in open Fair and not otherwise, and that no Horse, Mare or Gelding shall be sold at this Fair but what shall be duly vouched for and tolled.

GOD SAVE THE QUEEN

Dated this 9th day of September, 1976

BY ORDER,

M. H. F. HAMMOND,
CHIEF EXECUTIVE AND TOWN CLERK

Right: This 1976 poster details the royal charter antecedents of Nottingham's Goose Fair.

Below: The Goose Fair at Nottingham in full flow around 1910.

GOOSEFAIR NOTTINGHAM.   PHOTO. HENSON.

Hull Fair in Victorian times. Note the two policemen keeping watch in the foreground.

Suspended during the Great War, the fair underwent significant change in 1927 when a combination of work for a new headquarters building for Nottingham Council on the old Exchange site, and the laying of a tramway in the Great Market Square in the city centre, led to a shift in location to the out-of-town Forest site. This move prompted a protest, which was led by a leading showman, Pat Collins, but the council remained unmoved and the following year a new, bigger fair took place on the site, which remains to this day.

The Second World War also saw the Goose Fair suspended, but it returned, and despite having recently lost some of its ground to the building of the Nottingham Express Tramway, it continues to thrive. These days predominantly amusement-lead, the Goose Fair offers over 500 attractions, ranging from large rides to side stalls, or 'side stuff', as the showmen know them. It is also known for its food, with the traditional Goose Fair dish of mushy peas and mint joined these days by fare from all five continents.

It would be remiss to mention Nottingham without also mentioning Hull Fair, which takes place at around the same time, with the pair fighting it out for the title of the country's largest.

Priddy Fair

Priddy, a hilltop village in Somerset, held a sheep fair on the third Wednesday in August on the village green, with other days of the week being used for cattle and horses. It originated in 1352 when an outbreak of the Black Death in the city of Wells led to farmers seeking

Priddy Fair in the 1960s.

a new, safe location away from the pestilence. So, instead of holding the midsummer fair in the city centre, they moved to the isolated village in the Mendip Hills. This was only supposed to be a temporary measure but it was so popular that it never returned to Wells. Sadly, after 663 years, Priddy Sheep Fair was cancelled for the second year running in 2015 due to the high cost of road closures and policing, and the tradition now seems to have ended.

St Giles' Fair, Oxford

Fairs exist to entertain the public first, but the showmen who run them have their own favourites, and for most of them St Giles' Fair in Oxford is probably the best two-day street fair going. The last fair remaining of the five that have been held in the city, St Giles is also the youngest, having 'only' been going for nearly 500 years. The earliest dates back to 1122, when Henry I granted a charter to the Priory of St Frideswide, which opened on the Vigil and Day of the Translation of St Benedict and ran for five days.

Originally known as the St Giles' Wake, the fair is always held on the first Monday and Tuesday following the Sunday after the Feast of St Giles (1 September) and occupies the tree-lined roadway from St Giles Church down to the Martyrs Memorial by the church of St Mary Magdalen at the south end of the fair.

In the eighteenth century the fair became a toy fair, and in the following century a general children's fair. As transport improved, however, the fair was able to attract more

Crowds would swarm St Giles in Oxford during the annual fair.

Oxford's St Giles at night, with illumination allowing the crowds to continue to enjoy the fair.

visitors and a wider array of attractions started to be set up. Today there is a full range of rides, including Tommy Matthew's Rotor and Stevens' Lighthouse Slip (or helter-skelter) at the head of the fair by the war memorial, as well as numerous ghost trains and fun houses, two sets of Dodgems, stalls selling candy floss, toffee apples and toys down the middle, and at the far end Joey Noyce's Starflyer occupies the position previously held by his family's Gallopers. The showmen pull on at 5 a.m. on Sunday morning to build up, stopping at 10 a.m. for an hour, so as not to disturb church services, and pulling down starts as soon as the last ride stops on the Tuesday evening, and carries on all through the night, as the road must open to traffic first thing on Wednesday morning.

All rents and dues from the fair still go to St John's College and the City of Oxford Council, who, in conjunction with the Showmen's Guild, run the fair. When the fair is running, the ancient church of St Giles is always open to visitors for refreshments and has displays on the history of the fair.

Stourbridge Fair

The area known as Stourbridge Common on the outskirts of Cambridge was home to the largest fair in medieval Europe. In 1211, King John issued a charter giving the leper chapel at 'Steresbrigge' the right to hold a fair to finance a leper hospital, which had to be outside the city. The fair grew thanks to its location alongside the River Cam, which gives access to the Wash and the port of King's Lynn, and also adjoins the main road to Newmarket.

Visitors and traders flocked to the fair in their thousands from far and wide. Elizabeth I stated in a 1589 charter that the fair 'far surpassed the greatest and most celebrated fairs

The Midsummer Fair at Cambridge.

of all England'. The fair was vast, requiring every carpenter in Cambridge to construct the necessary booths, which were erected to form mini streets, with the traders sleeping inside the booths both for security purposes and because no accommodation was available for miles around. In the centre was the Duddery, a quadrangle housing the largest stalls, with a Maypole for dancing standing alongside a pulpit for Sunday sermons.

The University of Cambridge believed that they should receive some of the revenue from the fair and tensions arose between Town and Gown as both tried to assert their rights, leading to the Queen intervening in 1589, decreeing that the town council should run the fair with the university enforcing weights and measures and imposing fines on traders for presenting 'all that was sinful and distracting for students'. Asserting this right, the Vice-Chancellor ordered the theatre booths to be demolished in 1740.

The fair was open for several weeks every September, but by the eighteenth century it was in decline as urban development spread and shops superseded markets. The last fair was held in 1933 and consisted of just one brave trader with an ice-cream cart. The fair has now been superceded by a fair held on Midsummer Common in Cambridge.

Stratford Mop

Initially a hiring fair, Stratford Mop is held on 10 October, or Old Michaelmas Day. Originally, farm workers and labourers would contract for the year from October to late September, when the harvest was gathered in. Those looking for employment attended in their best clothes with a tuft of wool in the lapel if they were a shepherd or horse hair if they were a wagoner. Milkmaids would wear a tuft of cow hair and servants would hold a

Roasting a ox at Stratford's mop fair.

The annual mop at Stratford in the 1960s.

mop. Other established fairs with a history as 'mops' include Warwick, Banbury, Daventry, and Kings Norton.

Proclamation of the fair took place at the High Cross (now demolished), which was accompanied by the roasting of an In 2003 the district council wanted to move the fair out of the town streets into a recreation ground but this was opposed by the Showmen's Guild. A lawyer reviewed all relevant material including the original charters granted by Edward VI in 1553, James I in 1611 and Charles II in 1676, which stated that 'mops should be held within and through all places, streets, lanes, alleys and fields in the said borough of Stratford-on-Avon'. The fair could only be moved with the consent of the public, so a postal survey was held by the council and the public voted for the fair to stay in the town, where it is still very popular and well attended each year.

These examples give some sense of both the common themes enjoyed by many fairs, but also how much they can vary in practice according to their roots and individual traditions. The tingle of history mingled with the smells of food, smoke and oil, the sounds of screams, barkers, machinery, sirens and animals, and the sights of brightly coloured rides and people enjoying themselves are all universal themes that are woven into our collective memory.

3

Skating on Thin Ice

Traditional fairs offered a break from normal routine and often marked a significant point in the annual calendar, and as such were predictable, as it was known exactly what day they'd arrive and leave, while at the same time offering a sense of unpredictability once they got going. There was, however, an exception to this rule, as some fairs might appear spontaneously and maybe only once in a lifetime. These would contain all the elements of a traditional fair – markets, fun, excitement and a touch of skulduggery – but in addition would offer a greater sense of anarchy; a sense of 'anything goes'. These were the great Thames frost fairs.

While it was not unknown for the Thames to freeze over, there are accounts of it doing so as early as 250 AD, from the fifteenth century onwards it became less of a rarity. This can be explained by two phenomena, one natural and one man-made. Known as the 'Little Ice Age', this period was marked by particularly severe winters, during which temperatures plunged so low, and stayed there so long, that even the waters off the coast froze over. The man-made element was the old London Bridge, a feature of which was its closely spaced piers, which in turn were protected by large timber casings that were extended over time. The net result of this activity was a series of small gaps that ice floes from further up the river would effectively dam, leaving the river to still and freeze at ebb tide.

When the river did freeze it was initially regarded as a nuisance rather than a signal for frivolity. With the capital's main thoroughfare and distribution channel out of commission, fuel and food came into short supply, which, combined with the persistent low temperatures, led to starvation and death for many. However, those whose position in society meant that they didn't have to worry so much about such things were able to take advantage of the ice. King Henry VIII travelled from central London to Greenwich by sleigh along the river in 1536, and Queen Elizabeth I was reported to 'shoot at marks' on the ice, while small boys enjoyed mass football matches. Those brave enough would also take carriages on the ice, probably more through gritted teeth than through any sense of adventure.

While the river froze over a total of five times in the sixteenth century, the 1600s saw a total of ten solid freezings, and the first of these, in 1608, saw the first recorded frost fair, although there are some suggestions that some kind of fair took place in the freezing

THE GREAT FROST.

Cold doings in London, except it be at the
LOTTERIE.

With Newes out of the Country.

A familiar talke betwene a Country-man and
a Citizen touching this terrible Frost and the great Lotterie,
and the effects of them.

The Description of the Thames frozen ouer.

Printed at London for *Henry Goßon*, and are to be sold at the signe of the

An early Thames frost fair.

of 1564. A description of the 1608 fair from the chronicler Edmund Howes describes how ice would form on every ebb in December, but would then be taken away when the tide came in. However, the ice stayed between tides for five days in January, and people 'went boldly upon the ice in most parts'. He went on to describe how that boldness grew and 'some shot at prickers, others bowled and danced, with variable other pastimes'.

As a frozen river represented a removal of livelihood for many, it is perhaps not surprising that some took advantage of the situation to make a bob or two, and Howes records that 'many set up booths and standings upon the ice as fruit sellers, victuallers, that sold beers and wine, shoemakers and a barbers tent etc.'. As with fairs held on common land, there was a sense that the frozen river didn't belong to anyone, and that it was fair game, but this wasn't strictly the case. The profession most directly affected by a freezing were the ferrymen, and a feature of future frost fairs was the sight of ferrymen charging 2d or 3d for access to the ice, and also to carry people across it (though Howes doesn't mention it of 1608). Some reports were also made of channels being cut in the ice overnight, across which ferrymen would then charge to take people during the day.

The most renowned frost fair is probably that of 1683/4, during which the river was completely solid for two months to a depth of between 12 and 18 inches. The most famous chronicler of this freeze was John Evelyn, the writer, gardener and diarist, who was also a contemporary of Samuel Pepys, who labelled the event as 'the greate frost'. The first inklings of a frost fair came on 1 January, when booths began to be set up, forming 'streets', as tended to be the custom, with the main 'street' on this occasion being known as Broad Street or Temple Street. At some point a coach-and-four was driven across the ice as a wager to prove its resilience, and by the 6th the river was, indisputably, totally frozen over.

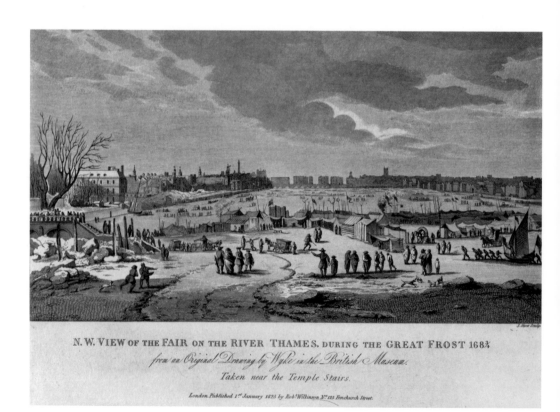

N.W. VIEW OF THE FAIR ON THE RIVER THAMES. DURING THE GREAT FROST 1683/4
from an Original Drawing by Wyke in the British Museum.
Taken near the Temple Stairs.

London. Published 1st January 1825 by Robt Wilkinson No 125 Fenchurch Street.

A view of the Thames frost fair of 1683/4. Note the 'streets'. (Yale Center for British Art, Paul Mellon Collection)

On the 9th, Evelyn bravely ventured his way on to the ice and over to the opposite bank. On another occasion he strolled from Westminster Steps to Lambeth Palace to dine with the Archbishop of Canterbury, walking from Lambeth Stairs to Horseferry on the way back. Evelyn described the streets of booths forming a mini-town, with horses and carriages plying up and down and even whole oxen being roasted. The entertainments on offer were diverse, and are best summed up in Evelyn's description of them as 'a Bacchanalian triumph of carnival on the water'.

So what might he have seen? Food and drink would have taken centre stage; not just roasted meats but also novelty foods such as spiced buns and apples, hot puddings, gingerbread, nuts and fruits – all at inflated prices due not just to their growing scarcity due to the lack of incoming boats, but also because being offered from ice commanded a premium. Mulled wine, brandy and cider would also have been prominent, as would be 'geneva' or gin in later fairs. Potential customers would be welcomed with the greeting 'What lack ye sir, beer, ale or brandy?', and it was said that 'folk do tipple without fear to sink, more liquor than the fish beneath do drink'. Meanwhile, all this would take place against a background of more traditional fairground entertainers such as fire-eaters, jugglers and sword swallowers.

While most would totter around on shoes, braver souls placed the leg bones of animals on their feet and strapped them to their ankles. Armed with an iron staff, they would then ski across the ice 'at a velocity equal to the flight of a bird, or bolt discharged from a crossbow.' Then, of course, there'd be the small boys who would delight in sliding along the ice and bumping people out of the way, as they still do today. Iron skates from Holland were a rarity at this time, but in later frost fairs all sorts of sports would also take place on the ice. Enterprising ferrymen would put their boats on wheels and charge to take people around, dodging the musicians, stilt-walkers and singers all trying to earn a crust. Carriages across the ice became so frequent that they even operated to a timetable.

For most of those who made their way onto the ice, a priority was some kind of souvenir, such as small trinkets or children's toys, which were labelled as being sold on the Thames. The most popular souvenir, however, was a memento from one of the printing presses, the first of which was operated by a printer called George Croom, who charged sixpence for a card with the customer's name, the date and the fact that the card was printed on the Thames. This was such a must-have item that even the king, the Merry Monarch Charles II, had one made, which was printed on a quarto of Dutch paper measuring 3.5 by 4 inches. Croom reputedly made £5 a day for printing relatively simple cards, and it was unsurprising that later fairs reported a number of printing presses – as many as ten, on one occasion.

There was undoubtedly a novelty value to venturing out onto the ice and, once you got your legs, doing something unusual once you got there. If a traditional fair offered a sense of being outside your normal comfort zone, a fair on ice offered the same and more, with a very real threat of injury (or even death) by falling at a time when having a broken bone set was no laughing matter. Surprisingly perhaps, reports of drownings were not unheard of and in later centuries the Icemen of the Royal Humane Society stood on guard to rescue those who'd ventured too far.

As Evelyn hinted, frost fairs were also an excuse for debauchery, which was perhaps fuelled by the sense that the temporary world operated by its own rules. In the absence of

The frozen Thames. Note the old London Bridge with its arches. (Yale Center for British Art, Paul Mellon Collection)

light, the river was especially dangerous at night, and even during the day visitors were well advised to stick to the tracks that had been worn into the ice, even as these became thinner. One observer noted 'bawds, whores, pickpockets, jilts and cheats', and in addition to gambling dens there were other places dedicated to 'the provision of more dubious, more fleshy diversions'.

The fair of 1683/4 was by no means the only great frost fair on the Thames, but in many ways it set the precedent for those that followed, a prerequisite to a comprehensive fair being a long period of frost and no ingress of water from London Bridge. Most freezings were too short to support a fair, while on other occasions the water that came in with the tide would fall over the ice dam on the bridge before freezing, forming great cliffs of irregular ice, described as if 'there had been a terrible storm and it had froze the waves just as they were beating against one another'.

There were other great fairs, in both 1715/6 and 1739/40, although during the latter a huge hole appeared in the ice and swallowed up tents, businesses and people. The river froze again in 1789, leading to another tragedy when a ship was anchored to a riverside pub in Rotherhithe – not next to the pub, but physically to it, with anchors being secured in the cellar and to a beam in the house. When loosening ice caused the boat to move around, it took out the beam of the house, which promptly collapsed, killing five people in their beds.

The frost of 1813/14 was labelled 'the frost of the century'. The main thoroughfare on the ice became known as City Road and an elephant was led across the Thames below Blackfriars Bridge. But the frost fairs' days were numbered. In 1831 the Old London Bridge was demolished and exchanged with Sir John Rennie's replacement, which had wider arches. This, combined with a warmer climate and the construction of the Thames

The frost fair in 1788/9. Note the masts of the frozen-in ships and the Tower of London. (Yale Center for British Art, Paul Mellon Collection)

The Thames Frost Fair of 1814.

Embankment thirty years later, which had the effect of channelling the river and making it go faster, meant the end of the Thames freezing, and with it the end of Thames frost fairs.

Their legacy continues, however, with the growing popularity of winter wonderland-type fairs in major city centres around Christmastime that evoke some of the atmosphere of those times, which include skating rinks, but perhaps lack much of the debauchery and sense of edginess and danger that was an essential element of the great frost fairs of old.

4

Holding on Tight

While the demise of the Thames frost fairs can be traced to highly specific causes, wider trends challenged the more traditional travelling fair. Some of these have already been touched upon, including changing tastes and technologies, increased urbanisation, better transport and growing sophistication in tastes. These accumulated to a point where, by the latter half of the nineteenth century, fairs were not only losing their popularity, but some of those in power were actively seeking to get rid of them altogether.

At the turn of the nineteenth century there had been no shortage of variety in what most fairgrounds had to offer. The majority of attractions in a typical market town fair would have been offered from individual booths, offering small toys, food or drink, as well as people such as cordwainers offering shoe repairs, fortune tellers, teeth-pullers and conjurors. Interspersed among these there might also be small, usually hand-turned, or occasionally horse-turned, rides constructed out of wood, or individuals singing (frequently obscene) ballads.

In larger fairs there would also be a few 'headline' attractions, which were usually shows. These shows might offer the opportunity to see something out of the ordinary, be it a 'freak' (real or manufactured) or simply someone from a different culture, such as the 'Red Indian' noted by Wordsworth at the 1815 Bartholomew Fair. Also popular were

A performing bear being paraded to publicise the fair.

Southwark Fair in 1796.
(Wellcome Library, London)

A quack doctor and a
dissenting parson selling
their respective goods.
(Wellcome Library, London)

So-called 'freaks' were always
popular, such as this tall man
and 'wonder midgets'.

performing animals, which ranged from small insect or bird menageries to the elephant seen at the 1813/14 Thames Frost Fair, although this was well out of the norm. Bear-baiting and cockfighting were also regular attractions.

A particular favourite during the early part of the nineteenth century was Toby the Sapient Pig, who was said to be able to 'spell and read, cast accounts, play at cards, tell a person what o'clock it is to the minute and tell the age of anyone in company', among other gifts. Toby was toured and trained by a magician and trainer called Hoare, who claimed Toby had even penned his own memoirs!

Even acknowledging the fact that it was one of the larger fairs, an account of the 1822 Bartholomew Fair is still revealing, listing five circus booths, four menageries and a number of theatres, peep shows, freak shows and glassblowing acts, alongside exhibition shows that typically included waxworks or illusions.

The fundamentals of the fair remained little changed for centuries. One reason for this was the constraints imposed on showmen by their transport options. In the earliest days,

'Toby the Sapient Pig – He will discover a person's thoughts!!'

38

Using four legs rather than two to transport shows became increasingly necessary to transport shows.

showmen would travel with their show on their back, with some later using barrows or carts. Horses became an option for the more successful, allowing them to transport shows, but they were, if anything, slower, needing to stop for rests and feeds. Horses did have the advantage of being able to pull a living van though, allowing showmen to travel with their wives and family, who could also help with the show. While there was some innovation in what was offered, the pace of change was outstripped by that taking place in society in general, leaving the travelling fair in danger of becoming staid and old hat.

One of the greatest showmen of his time, 'Lord' George Sanger epitomises how showmen rose to this challenge, and in an era defined by its monarch, it is perhaps fitting that he claimed that the first act of his long career took place the day of Victoria's Coronation in June 1838. By looking at Sanger's career, we can gain an insight into how the fair developed during this period of rapid change in the nation. Before going any further it is worth noting that both this claim, and indeed his adoption of a title, offer perfect examples of the most basic attribute of the showman – showmanship. Sanger's first day may have been the day of the Coronation, but true or not, it made for a good story. What is known is that his first professional foray into the life of the fair was as a 'patterer' for Malabar the Juggler, and that Sanger never received a peerage from his monarch.

George was the son of James Sanger, who had learned conjuring tricks while in the Royal Navy, and used these to become a showman after his discharge. Once on the road, he developed a peep show that featured the Battle of Trafalgar, which he claimed to have fought in, and 'human curiosities'. One of ten children, George was expected to help with the show as the family travelled the fair circuit, gaining an education of sorts during the quiet months over winter like so many showmen's children. The end of the Napoleonic Wars and the hard times that followed led many to adopt a travelling life, and many showmen dynasties can trace their origin to these times, with Sanger being a good example of children becoming part of the 'family business' for want of any viable alternative.

A feature of George's life was what we would now call entrepreneurialism, but it can also be interpreted as the ability to adapt to circumstances – the hallmark of any successful showman. Lessons were often learned the hard way, and when Malabar the Juggler fled without paying him, young George branched out on his own, initially selling confectionary and later exhibiting canaries and white mice he had trained to perform tricks such as firing a cannon or walking a tightrope.

In 1849 George married a lion tamer from Wombwell's circus, having spent a year travelling the country with his brothers to raise enough money to do so. Unsure whether his prospects were better on the road or operating from a single site, George, like many showmen, chanced his arm at the Great Exhibition of 1851. Here they suffered from the showmen's curse of bad weather all summer, with the site becoming a quagmire. Disillusioned, he went back on the road, where he experienced all the travails of the travelling showman, which he later recorded in his autobiography *Seventy Years a Showman*. These included bolting horses, fights, raids, riots and even how on one occasion he had to carry on with his show despite losing an infant son, needing the money he raised to pay for the funeral. These tales were leavened, however, by explanations of a few showmen's tricks.

A staple of George's show during this time remained the peep show. An attraction that could trace its origins back to the fifteenth century, this popular entertainment allowed a customer or punter to view a scene, or series of scenes, which were usually etched onto glass or a mirror, through a small hole. As well as offering entertainment, these could often be the only way someone could gain an appreciation of a major event such as a battle or the funeral of a monarch in the days before newspapers and moving pictures.

George understood the importance of putting on a show, and it has been suggested that he got his 'Lord' epithet from his father, who mockingly called him 'your Lordship' because of his sharp dressing. He also retained his facility with animals and, along with his brothers, moved more into circus acts, starting with a Welsh Pony bought for £7. This move reflected a general drift away from the sorts of shows offered at the turn of the century towards greater spectacle. What might have seemed miraculous to farm workers who rarely left their parish would appear laughable to a more cynical and knowing urban audience. Wooden hand-cranked rides, waxworks, peep shows and menageries were no longer enough to get large crowds to part with their money and, along with growing

'Lord' George Sanger's Hall and Zoological Gardens in 1885.

bawdiness, this was a contributing factor towards many fairs ceasing to operate around the middle of the century – not just Bartholomew Fair, but those at Camberwell, Greenwich and Stepney in London alone.

Taking a show indoors meant it could be held for longer and become more elaborate, and with this purchase the Sangers reflected a wider trend to create zoos rather than travelling menageries, as well as for acts such as conjurors and illusionists to migrate to the alternative circuit of the music halls. Sanger continued until 1905, but by then competition had become so fierce that he was forced to sell off most of his show and retire to his winter quarters. He died six years later in violent circumstances, when he was mortally injured by an ex-employee during a robbery.

At the height of his fame, Sanger had also become active in championing the rights of showmen. These had come under threat during the 1880s by an MP named George Smith, who, showing true Victorian zeal for order, wanted to restrict the movements of travelling people. Following success in limiting the movement of bargees four years previously, he introduced the Moveable Dwellings Bill in 1888. As well as imposing regulations on the number of people allowed to live in a living wagon, the Bill proposed powers for local authorities to inspect dwellings. Needless to say, this was unpopular with the proud showmen's fraternity and, accordingly, Smith was chased through the streets when he attended the Birmingham Onion Fair.

In 1889 a number of travelling people who operated fairground shows and rides held a meeting at the Black Lion Hotel in Salford, Manchester. They had been invited there by Mr Pedgrift, the publisher of the theatrical newspaper *The Era*, who was concerned about George Smith's Bill. This led to the creation of the Van Dweller's Association, with menagerie operator J. W. Bostock being elected as the first president. Two years later, they were led by the Reverend Thomas Horne, who had started his career as a showman in his father's show dressed up in a bear outfit and kicking up his legs shouting 'Sugar' on his father's command, and later running a penny bazaar around the Lancashire Wakes, before training to become a priest in Rotherham. In 1900 the association was reconstituted as a trade protection association for showmen and became known as the Showmen's Guild, and 'Lord' George Sanger himself took over as president until 1908. Like workers elsewhere in Victorian Britain, showmen had discovered the power of collective action. No longer a loose collection of mavericks, showmen had become – in part at least – like everyone else.

Although being a showman had always been a hard life, during these times they were particularly looked down upon by the authorities, being spoken of in the same breath as gypsies, thieves and vagrants. Not having property or a fixed address stood them apart – as did not having a visible means of support. It also didn't help that many places hosting travelling fairs tended to experience a rise in teenage pregnancies when they visited.

It comes as no surprise, therefore, that they were regarded with suspicion and not always dealt with fairly, it being difficult for outsiders to distinguish between showmen and the bad sorts who undoubtedly did make a living from crowds who attended the fair. When times were hard, showmen occasionally needed to resort to desperate measures such as 'thimble-rigging', a variation of the three-card trick delivered using three thimbles and a pea, and such activities, alongside frequent night-time brawls (Sanger describes many such rows in his book) and the perceived 'corruption' of working men's morals all contributed to undermining the respectability of show families.

The apparent desire among the Victorian elite to protect the morals of the working classes – a term that was loosely interpreted to cover a range of patrician concerns – also led to the conversion of open spaces into landscaped parks, which removed traditional fair sites. With less concern for the impact upon their workers, landowners also created enclosures of common land where they hadn't already done so, further depriving fairs of traditionally used sites. Expanding towns also needed the space that was occupied on an occasional basis by fairs, which was no doubt encouraged in some cases by the benefit to the municipal purse of being relieved of the burden of policing them.

Aided by the Fairs Act of 1871, which, in a phrase that perhaps revealed the presiding mood of the time, stated that 'fairs are unnecessary, are the cause of grievous immorality and are very injurious to the inhabitants of towns where they are held', local authorities could close fairs so long as there was no public demand for them, placing a further onus upon showmen to lobby for their retention. Furthermore, this was also a time when political radicalism was an ongoing concern for the authorities, and occasions that would allow large gatherings of the working classes were generally frowned upon. This was all the more so if those occasions included stages where satirical plays mocking the establishment could be performed, as was often the case at fairs.

As the century progressed, alternative entertainments such as music halls, travelling exhibitions and lantern shows competed with the fairs for entertainment revenue, making life even harder for showmen. Potential audiences had also become more mobile, and although some railway companies put on 'funfair specials', they were also doing

A children's pedal-powered ride from 1904.

42

this for a range of other attractions as the public began to enjoy a much wider choice of entertainment. Following the demise of Bartholomew Fair in 1855, as well as other long-established fairs, it became increasingly clear that showmen needed to up their game if they were to remain relevant, which probably explains why they were among the first to see the potential of the new wonder of the age – steam.

Jumbo-powered – pulling a load on to Hull Fair.

Anderton & Rowland's show from 1905.

5

Steaming Ahead

The first steam-powered roundabouts made their debut at the Bolton New Year Fair and the Midsummer Fair at Halifax in the 1860s. Credit for being the first to present a steam-powered ride is usually given to roundabout proprietor Thomas Bradshaw, with the engine being made by Rogerson & Brimelow of Deansgate and Bradshaw patenting the idea in 1863. Despite safety concerns should the engine explode (particularly relating to that of children), it soon became clear to watching showmen that this new technology had the potential to revolutionise the fair, not just in the range of rides they could offer, but also in the development of steam engines that would allow them to transport larger shows from ground to ground.

A period of innovation began, with Bradshaw's ride being followed by another steam-powered roundabout presented by Sidney Soames at Aylsham Fair in 1865. At the forefront of this period of innovation was Frederick Savage of King's Lynn. Originally a manufacturer of agricultural machinery, Savage dedicated himself to making fairground rides, selling three-abreast Gallopers as early as the mid-1860s that led in time to four-abreast rides with a total of fifty-six horses, including his patented 'platform slide', which saw the horses swing out when they gained speed. By the 1870s, Savage was supplying steam rides called Velocipedes, which were circles of cast-iron bicycles. A key breakthrough was the development of a steam engine mounted on a sprung truck, in which a crown wheel and pinion engaged with a centre hub, from which spokes could radiate.

The basic principle of the powered roundabout formed the basis of many new rides, with Savage sometimes coming up with the idea for a new ride that others then improved on, and sometimes coming up with ways to improve someone else's idea. He was also open to collaboration, as with the 'Sea-On-Land' – a ride with boats complete with sails, each named after leading liners of the day, that pitched and tossed as if at sea, which he developed in partnership with William Sanger. Such became Savage's renown that his company began to host an annual dinner for showmen at the Duke's Head in King's Lynn during the Mart Fair. He went on to become Lord Mayor of King's Lynn and on 27 May 1892 a statue was erected in his honour at the spot where he waved to showmen when they entered town.

Other steam-powered rides during this era included Steam Yachts, utilising upright cylinders, patented in 1888 by William Cartwright of Bromwich; Switchbacks, which

Above: A horse in shafts being used to steer Burrell No. 2802 owing to a breakdown of the steering mechanism.

Below: Hand-turned overboats, such as these on Hampstead Heath, were to become a thing of the past.

OVER-BOATS
ON HAMPSTEAD HEATH.

A set of steam-driven
Gallopers, restored by
the late John Carter.

Savage's Sea-on-Land.

A Savage engine in
action today.

Savage patented in the same year; Tunnel Railways; and the Razzle-Dazzle, in which customers sat on a circular platform and dipped from side to side as the ride rotated. These new rides revitalised the fairground, bringing them back from the brink to a point where there were 200 fairs in towns and villages across the land every weekend between Easter and November. This growing popularity had saved them and the authorities, whose focus had previously been on how to close them down, shifted their attention to regulation in an acknowledgement that they were here to stay.

Above left: Frederick Savage's statue, standing where he used to greet the showmen as they made their way to King's Lynn Mart.

Above right: An Edwardian freak show. 'Beautiful Minnie' – take a peek for a penny.

Right: *Sunny Boy Number 2,* owned by Marshall & Sons, seen pulling the loads.

Penzance's Corpus Christi Fair in 1926, showing Anderton & Rowlands' fleet of showmen's engines.

Traylen's *Marina* at Hampton Court Fair, 1935.

Around the turn of the century, showmen once again demonstrated their ability to spot and adapt to a new trend by presenting Bioscopes – a form of early cinema. These were first seen at the season-opener King's Lynn Mart in 1897, being presented by Randall Williams, the 'King of the Showmen'. These shows introduced moving pictures to those not living in towns and cities and proved to be an instant hit. From 1902 onwards, Bioscope shows, with their large fronts, began to travel using traction engines, often being broken down into six or seven loads. Using a dynamo attached to the smoke box, these then also provided the power to produce better illumination for the show itself, as well as lights around the front of the show. The front would also be dominated by a large pipe organ, which was used to attract people and entice them in to see the otherwise hidden show, acting as an alternative to the until-then traditional megaphone.

Organs became a feature of the fairground, helping to transform the atmosphere, with the best organs coming from France and Holland and being made by firms such as Gavioli or Marenghi. These were huge machines with intricate carvings that were attractions in themselves, with the largest, such as Orchastrophones, having over a hundred keys. Loud

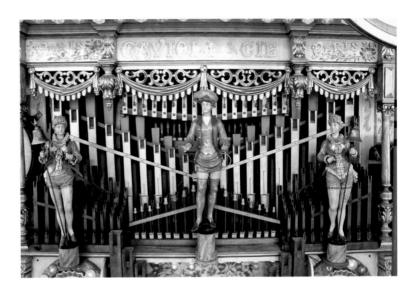

A Gavioli organ
on Noyce's
Savage Gallopers.

The Razzle
Dazzle in
preservation
at Holycombe.

music created an atmosphere in a tradition that continues to this day, with changing tastes in music helping to define different eras of the fairground, while lighting from the generators on the traction engines meant that showmen could continue to operate, and take money, well past dusk.

Whereas previously rides and side attractions used to close when the sun fell, leaving drinking dens and other less savoury attractions to take centre stage, with electric lighting (and especially changing colours) the show went on, becoming more exciting, if anything. Gone were the unpleasant smells and fire risks of tallow and naphtha, and their successor, carbon arc lighting, allowed for the introduction of spot lighting, with the constant power offered by mounted generators having a transformative effect. The adoption of steam to make electricity had the effect of making funfairs feel like they were part of the future, as well as safer to visit at night, which attracted back some of the audience they had lost towards the end of the nineteenth century.

Fairgrounds could now stand their own against rival attractions, such as music halls; luring the public in with the thrill of movement and an assault on their senses, while offering a three-dimensional experience. At the same time, the growing working class had more money to spend, and where better to spend it than at the fairground? As well as more money, working men also had more time with the Factory Act of 1850 having made Saturdays a half day for work, and the 1871 Bank Holidays Act creating four Bank Holidays on Easter Monday, Whit Monday, the first Monday in August and Boxing Day.

While the basic function of the charter fairs remained – with many mop fairs still being used for hiring, for example – rides were now the main attraction. By 1907, rides outnumbered shows by two to one at Hull Fair, and two years later saw the first Cakewalk, named after a dance popular at the time, which was comprised of two parallel oscillating walkways powered by the steam engine, so if the music was speeded up the ride followed, creating a 'let's have a go ourselves' spectacle. Rides were becoming bigger and more adventurous as steam mitigated the constraint of transport. While a horse might be able to pull one wagon, a traction engine could pull three or four, and the sight of a road-train of these machines, as well as the brightly and ornately decorated showmen's living vans, would form a moving advertisement for the fair coming to town.

One of the first such engines to be ordered direct from the manufacturer by a showman was the Burrell No. 1451 *Monarch*, which was built in 1889 by Burrell's of Thetford, who became known for their trademark 'Lake Crimson' colour with 'Deep Yellow' wheels. Showmen would customise the engines using gold leaf, with scrollwork being particularly popular. With increasing takings, showmen could afford to invest in these new engines (although initially it was only the richer showmen who could afford them), and these pioneers had to experiment with just how big a load an engine could usefully pull.

Credit was becoming easier to obtain from banks, or from the manufacturers of engines and rides themselves, allowing for further investment. In time, second-hand engines came on to the market, spreading the base of ownership. With steam engines, life on the road became less precarious and less vulnerable to a particularly bad spell of weather (although this particular vulnerability has never quite gone away altogether), or to freak accidents such as a horse bolting or going lame.

Some showmen started to lease sites from local corporations, and then sub-let plots to others, having reserved the best sites for themselves. As rides grew in size, space itself became shorter in supply, especially in the expanding towns, leading to inevitable hikes in rent. Although showmen had always been entrepreneurs, they were now, more than ever, businessmen too, and businessmen with interests to protect. With the threat of George Smith's Private Members Bill finally put to bed after five years of resistance in the mid-1890s, showmen saw the advantage of banding together. Following on from the foundation of the Van Dwellers Protection Association, which became the Showmen's Guild in 1910, the British Roundabout Proprietors & Showmen's Union (later known as 'the Combine') formed around the turn of the century, with smaller operators joining regional bodies. It is also from around this time that some of today's great showmen dynasties can trace their predecessors.

6

Riding a Switchback

Steam had revitalised the fair, laying the groundwork for the attraction-based entertainment we know today, but the first half of the twentieth century was to provide two more significant challenges, both in the form of war. If the evolution of the fair in preceding centuries (at least until the coming of steam) had been like a gentle roundabout, albeit one running out of momentum, then the two global conflagrations and their aftermath would mean that the ride from here on was to be more like a switchback.

The devastation in terms of young men's lives, and on the economy, of the Great War was to prove a major shock to showmen. The appetite for frivolity disappeared for the time being, and the Showmen's Guild found itself having to convince corporations of the need to reopen fairs that had been shut down during hostilities. On a practical level, peace brought with it a desperate shortage of manpower, which in turn led to a rise in wages, from £2 a week for a skilled man before the war, to nearer £4–£5 after it. The cost of purchasing rides also rose – in the case of a Scenic Railway, for example, prices went up from £3,000 to £9,000 – and the cost of traction engines doubled.

Despite the war accelerating the development of diesel engines, steam remained the form of power of choice for showmen who were unable to invest in wholescale change, especially while coal remained so abundant. As such, the fundamentals of the fair remained the same after the war, even though the rumblings of change could be detected by those for an ear for it. New rides were introduced in the 1920s, many of which have remained features of the fairground to this day, including Chairoplanes, Waltzers and that perennial favourite, the Dodgems.

The Dodgem as we know it now was probably introduced by the Lusse Brothers in 1928, although there were patents for similar concepts earlier than this. They took off when the idea of the moveable, steerable car was introduced, and the rides were manufactured by the likes of Orton & Spooner, Lang Wheels and Rytecraft. Whatever their antecedents, the Dodgems offered another good example of showmen picking up on the latest public fascination – in this case cars – with the Dodgem car probably being the closest most people would ever get to 'being behind the wheel'.

Shortly before this, the public had been treated to the British Empire Exhibition, which was opened on St George's Day 1924 by King George V primarily to showcase trade within

Petrol was starting to take over from steam.

Witching Waves, the Imperial International Exhibition in 1909.

The Dodg'Em at the Kursaal Gardens, Southend.

'It's Great Fun At Butlin's
Amusement Park!'

The Whip at Blackpool.

'The Joys of Wembley'.
A poster promoting the
British Empire Exhibition.

The Amusement Park at Wembley during the British Empire Exhibition.

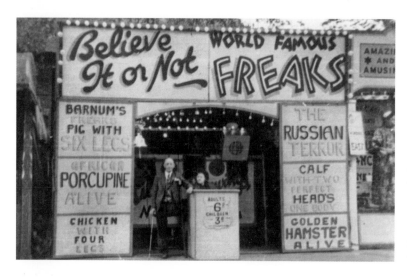

Freak shows were still popular with the crowds, although these freaks were mainly pictures rather than 'real' thing.

The Joy Wheel – the rage of two continents.

Learning to fly after the First World War.

the Empire, but also featured a large amusement park on a summer-long site. Held at Wembley, on what had been a greenfield site, the exhibition was home to the world's first bus station, which was able to handle 100,000 visitors a day, and the location also had good rail links. The population was now mobile and eager to have fun, and showmen were able to provide it through a combination of popular new rides and shows, including a water chute and an aerial display of aircraft picked out with spotlights at night in a show called 'London Defended'. The fair was so successful that it was repeated the following year, attracting 10 million visitors on top of the 17 million who'd visited in the first year.

Travelling fairs remained popular with the public during the 1920s, with new shows such as the Wall of Death supplementing more traditional roundabouts, while attractions such as the Bioscope, waxworks and menageries found themselves replaced with shows such as Wild West spectaculars, pioneered by the Shufflebottom family, and dancing or parading shows featuring scantily clad (or often unclad) beauties. The authorities retained their wariness towards the fairs, however, and Medical Officers would regularly inspect showmen's living vans during mop fairs in order to test for infectious diseases, with cholera being a particular concern.

Wembley had demonstrated the benefits of static fairs, as well as bigger rides, and it was during this period that amusement parks, which were often located on the coast, raised their game. The king was the Blackpool Pleasure Beach, with the town offering not just an

Blackpool Pleasure Beach showing Maxim's Flying Machine in the 1900s.

The Virginia Reel at Blackpool.

amusement park, including a scenic railway rollercoaster, but the sea, piers and theatres, all of which were lit up at night by electric illuminations. Good railway links made Blackpool particularly popular with those enjoying breaks from work during various wakes weeks from different mill towns around Lancashire.

Other static fairs existed in places such as Dreamland in Margate, Barry Island outside Cardiff, the Kursaal in Southend and the Spanish City in Whitley Bay, Tyne and Wear. These parks were sometimes labelled as 'Pleasure Gardens', harking back to the large gardens used for promenading and often romantic liaisons, which had been particularly popular in the eighteenth century. Initially for the well off, as time went on these gardens attracted all sorts, who were drawn to the shows, acrobats, tightrope walkers and fireworks offered, with the parks coming into their own at night. These static fairs were not unique to the UK, with the Tivoli Gardens in Copenhagen, which traced its origin to 1843, and the Prater in Vienna offering earlier examples in Europe.

An Art Deco front to John Hoadley's Waltzer at the Spanish City, Whitley Bay.

In 1927 a new static park was opened by the showman Billy Butlin in Skegness, sowing the seeds for a wider dream that was to revolutionise entertainment for working people in the following years. Butlin had come to the UK after the war and invested £4 in a stall at his uncle's fair. He soon learned that making it easier to win a prize increased takings, and he was soon earning enough to buy new stalls and other fairground equipment. Soon enough he could travel in his own right, and opened his Skegness Fair. Continued growth brought him to the point where he could realise his dream of adding accommodation to his static fair and create the first 'holiday camp' in 1936.

For working families on a budget, the idea of an 'all in' price – an early form of 'package deal', covering accommodation, food and entertainment, which included the static fair – was particularly attractive, as was the provision of childcare, allowing parents to enjoy themselves of an evening. A respected showman, Butlin's energy, vision and commitment (it was said he would never ask anyone to do something he wouldn't do himself, from cleaning a toilet to riding on the Wall of Death) was to serve him well, and he followed up on the success of Skegness with a second camp at Clacton two years later. He had plans for a third at Filey, but these were put on hold by another world war.

Like its predecessor, the Second World War had an immediate impact upon the fair, although some kept going through initiatives largely driven by the Showmen's Guild, such as 'Holidays at Home' and 'Blackout Fairs'. Steam engines came back into their own as coal remained unrationed and other combustibles remained available, with engines thundering back to the fair at night after being used to pull down damaged buildings with their winches during the day time.

Things were tough, and peace brought with it fresh challenges. Many pre-war rides needed too much investment to be returned to service, and instead ex-War Department equipment such as searchlight trailers were adapted to make new rides. Steam, meanwhile, now seemed to belong to another era, and traction engines were gradually replaced by diesel-powered ex-Army Scammells and Diamond Ts.

Although over 1,000 showmen served in the armed forces, the loss of manpower was nowhere near as bad as after the Great War, and not shutting down completely during hostilities meant that by the end of the 1940s there was a sense that showmen had weathered the worst, and some better than others. Ever the enterprising showman, Billy Butlin had persuaded the army to complete his Filey site and build two others at Ayr and Pwllheli as training camps, before reclaiming them after the war. Four others followed, and soon Bultins, along with Warners, became synonymous with holidays and fun.

A Skymaster ride, which was made out of aircraft drop tanks and a searchlight trailer, after the Second World War.

NAT CODONA'S SUPER AUTODROME

Kelvin Hall Glasgow 1946-7.

Nat Codona's Super Autodrome at Kelvin Hall, Glasgow, also just after the war.

58

Battersea Park Funfair, born out of the Festival of Britain.

Noble's new Rotor at Newcastle Town Moor in 1953.

Following in the footsteps of the British Empire Exhibition, the Festival of Britain, held in 1951, was established as a celebration and an attempt to put the war behind the nation by stressing optimism for the future. Exhibits at the main site on the South Bank focused on topics such as advances in science and architecture, and an amusement park was set up in Battersea, partly as a lighter alternative. The park continued to operate after the Festival closed, operating a pay gate in order to generate funds to help offset the costs of the Festival, which was a cause of controversy during a time of austerity.

Encouraged by the government, who even provided £30,000 for purpose, showmen were encouraged to look to the US for exciting new attractions, and seven new rides opened at the Festival. Showman John Collins presented a Big Dipper, inside of which he presented a Brooklands Speedway, a Dragon Mountain next to it, and the Todd family's Wall of Death inside. One of the American imports was a Jets ride consisting of eight arms with two-seater planes on the end that raised and lowered, with riders performing stunts such as rollovers. The biggest attraction at the park was probably the Rotor, which was presented by Max Myers and built by Orton & Spooner of Burton upon Trent.

The fairground was changing, but also reflecting changing tastes. Old steam organs playing Glenn Miller tunes were replaced by loudspeakers blaring out Buddy Holly and Elvis Presley, which chimed with the atmosphere of the modern fairground. Rock 'n' Roll was a harbinger of a new age; one where the young had money and freedom and where there was more choice generally. Rationing had ended and the consumer age had arrived, and with it yet another challenge for showmen – television.

During the second half of the 1950s this new medium made the living room the location of choice for evening entertainment, with episodes of *Dixon of Dock Green* launched to offer competition to the new ITV service, attracting audiences of nearly 14 million by the turn of the decade, and *Coronation Street* on the commercial channel attracting over 20 million by 1964. Furthermore, wakes weeks and factory trips, a staple source of trade for fairgrounds over the decades, were becoming a thing of the past as jet travel heralded the beginning of foreign package holidays, which were seen as altogether more exciting than a week at a Butlin's holiday camp in Skegness or Bognor.

Fairs became the domain of teenagers and those in their early twenties as the baby boomers reached adolescence and compulsory National Service ended, the last call-up having come in December 1960. Full employment meant that the young had money in their pocket and leisure time to spend, and as the middle classes and families remained inside watching their TV screens, it's no surprise that showmen focused on teenagers for trade. The sounds of the Beatles and the Rolling Stones would fill the air, coming from stacked-up autochange record players suspended from the ceiling of the paybox by four bungie straps, with 45s now having replaced the more fragile 78s, and being amplified through the latest valve Panotrope, or amplifier. Even the young eventually grow up and gain responsibilities of their own, however, and as the 1960s went on, the fair needed fresh energy if it was to survive.

G. Ryan & Sons' Highflyer HMS *Victory* at Sefton Park, Liverpool in 1953.

Bowman's Jolly Jersey Bounce, Victoria Park, Hackney, in 1955.

Moving with the times.

7

Forwards and Backwards

Over the years, showmen had proven their resilience and ability to adapt to new trends, technologies and demands, and in so doing managed to keep the fair relevant to the times. It came as some surprise, therefore, that the next big thing was a hundred years old and had already been the fair's saviour once before – steam.

In 1964, the Friendship Circle of Showland Fans – a group of fairground enthusiasts founded in the early war years to document and keep the memory of old steam attractions – held a major steam fair at Shottesbrook Park in White Waltham, near Maidenhead. The fair went on for three days and attracted over 200,000 visitors who admired an impressive collection of steam engines, Steam Yachts, a Bioscope, Gallopers and numerous fairground organs. The rally was not the first of its kind – Woburn Abbey had held steam rallies since 1957 – but it was the biggest, and as such holds some claim to sparking the beginning of what we'd now regard as the fairground heritage movement, and creating a powerful impetus for those interested in preserving and restoring old steam equipment.

The 1971 Stratford-upon-Avon Edwardian Steam Fair, showing the extent to which the steam revival took grip.

Edward's Ben-Hur Speedway at Warwick Steam Fair in 1971.

Harry Wigfield's Noah's Ark and Coronation Speedway.

Tom Norman's Bioscope Show at Melton Old Tyme Steam Fair in 1965.

Steam was still very much in the public consciousness, as demonstrated in the popular 1962 film *The Iron Maiden* about a traction engine race, and by the fact that British Rail continued to operate steam engines up until 1968. At the same time, there was an understanding that steam's days were coming to an end and that it belonged to a different era. The future seemed to belong to new technologies such as atomic power and the space race, most particularly to the young, who were learning how to enjoy new freedoms and spending power. Understandably, fairs pitched themselves accordingly, playing the music of the 'beat generation' and trying to keep up with changing trends and tastes, such as offering rocket rides, for example.

It was to prove an uphill battle though, as the baby boomers settled into respectability during the 1970s and the entertainment market became increasingly competitive. The fair seemed to lose some of its gloss. When a fair came to town in the 1950s and '60s it had felt like a liberating army, but by the 1970s it carried a less positive air. While it had always been true that those visiting a fair had to have their wits about them, this sense intensified as the decade went on and, as had happened before in its history, more respectable types

A set of Savage's Gallopers built around 1884 with a 48 keyless organ at Bressingham Gardens, Diss, in Norfolk.

The Great Dorset Steam Fair, which is still going today.

and families drifted away. Things weren't helped by extreme weather, with heatwaves in 1975 and 1976 being followed by a run of particularly wet summers. Added to the mix were concerns about safety. In 1972, the Battersea Amusement Park, which had been taken over by a private company after the Festival of Britain, suffered a well-publicised and tragic accident on its Big Dipper, in which five died – an incident that highlighted the absence of systemic testing of fairground rides.

Meanwhile, the modern enemy, television, upped its game by introducing colour transmissions, with both the BBC and ITV showing all their programmes in colour by the end of the 1960s and the majority of households having sets capable of receiving it by the mid-1970s. The sedate charms of the snooker show *Pot Black*, as well as being able to see familiar favourites such as *Z-Cars* and *Doctor Who* in colour, proved to be enough to keep the British public in their homes at night when the fair came visiting.

Good fronts pull in the crowds – as do striptease shows and 'naughty' semi-clad girls.

The 'Voodoo Girl' performs 'the kiss of death'.

The Ashby Statutes Funfair in the 1960s – a classic street fair.

The 1970s was also an unhappy time for the economy, as epitomised by the three-day week in 1974, although many showmen demonstrated their resourcefulness during this crisis by hiring out their generators (showmen being one of the few groups using them), with some making enough money out of the crisis to buy new rides. This ability to turn a problem into an opportunity was repeated after the hurricane in 1987, when showmen were able to use their equipment to clear fallen trees.

Taken together, these trends were enough to cause what showmen call 'private business' – the sort of travelling fair that might pull into a local recreation ground – to struggle, and although the large Charter Fairs such as Hull and Nottingham still did reasonably well, some bigger names in the showmen's fraternity retired around this time, with others opting to sell up and buy permanent amusement arcades on the coast. Those who stayed had to adapt to meet the times. Parading shows with naked women sporting strategically placed tassels they were able to twirl in different directions had become passé, and although they might still be well received at a race meet, they became unacceptable at a regular town fair.

Young people were defying 'the system', sporting mohicans and listening to punk music, while the equally rebellious reggae of Bob Marley resounded around the fairground. Furthermore, if the young were challenging the status quo, so too were others in society in general, albeit in a gentler way. A backlash against the uniformity of consumerism and a concern for what might have been lost was gathering momentum, with the early 1970s seeing the launch of the Campaign for Real Ale and movements for 'real' bread. There seemed to be a desire to hark back to the past, to authenticity and 'heritage', and all that was associated with it. Family trips out reflected this, with membership of the National

Large charter fairs such as the Nottingham Goose Fair continued to retain their popularity.

Jolly Tubes as a space shuttle.

Trust, for example, doubling in the first half of the 1970s, and then again to over a million by the end of the decade. The perceived loucheness and cynicism of the fair did not seem to chime with this sentiment.

At a time when showmen were finding it difficult to find an audience, things were also getting tighter for them on the cost side. Red diesel, the lifeblood of the fair, had been almost as cheap as water in the 1960s, but this changed with the tripling of oil prices in the early 1970s. Add in the need for public liability insurance, taxation, rising rents and wages, and the economics of running a fair were tough. The days of being able to pay a gaff lad (the casual labour of the fair) a fiver and a corned beef sandwich, known to showmen as 'scran', and expecting them to sleep in a 'kip truck' or bellybox had well and truly passed. Equally, some of the practices of the past, such as gaff lads 'tapping', or short-changing, punters who presented a note, were no longer acceptable.

An answer lay in connecting with the growing taste for nostalgia. Rallies such as that held at White Waltham a decade earlier gained in popularity, and some showmen began to major on the steam fair element of their show. One such was John Carter, who bought a set of steam Gallopers in need of restoration in 1977, which he and his wife Anna subsequently travelled with to steam rallies. A Chair-o-Plane and some vintage side stuff were added, along with some Steam Yachts, forming the nucleus of a travelling fair in its own right. This has since gone from strength to strength, being presented by John and Anna's children after John's early death in 2000, with restoration workshops and a winter yard appropriately adjacent to the White Waltham airfield.

Another name of note during this time was Harry Wigfield, a fairground enthusiast who had a successful business making sheds and prefabricated bungalows. Showmen would come to him to make replacement parts for rides, and in 1969 he and his partner Les Enston formed Armroyd Lane, a company focused on restoring old fairground rides.

Carter's Steam Yachts in action.

Carter's Chair-o-Plane, decorated by Anna Carter.

Carter's Steam Fair.

A children's ride at
Carter's Steam Fair.

Carter's Jungle Thriller.

Their first venture was a 38-foot-diameter Jungle Safari Speedway Ark, which they sold after one season and replaced with an ex-Harry Gray-operated Lakin Coronation Speedway dating back to 1937. This was worked for four seasons before being sold to a Canadian showman in 1975. Armroyd Lane rebuilt a number of rides such as a Speedway, Gallopers, a Waltzer, a Twist and a set of Swinging Gyms, as well as a Royal Coronation Speedway, which ran for twenty-one years and is now at Folly Farm in Pembrokeshire. Harry Wigfield was also known for his Edwardian Steam Fair at Stratford-upon-Avon, which became a showcase for restored rides. Another example of the revival of steam around this time was the Great Dorset Steam Fair, which was founded by Michael Oliver and first held in 1969 at Stourpaine Bushes, then going under the name of the Great Working of Steam Engines.

Fairs began to fill with the sound of organs and the smell of steam engines once again, and the rides took on a more retro feel. The wholesale scrapping of steam engines ceased and old equipment was rediscovered in showmen's yards and restored. Fairs regained some of their lost attraction to families by tapping into the nostalgia market, not only through the rides themselves, but also by using the vehicles and living wagons as part of the show. This had been the case before, but it was now done explicitly, with information boards giving the history of vehicles, allowing parents and grandparents to reminisce to younger audiences about the anticipation and excitement they had associated with the fair when they were growing up. Fairs regained some of their lost respectability while at the same time an emphasis on steam opened up the possibility of opening for two days, including Sunday, allowing showmen to extend their earning capability.

Use of steam wasn't the only expression of this trend of taking back fairs to how they used to be, with some ancient fairs that had been closed down during the nineteenth century being revived. An example of this was the reopening of Charlton Horn Fair in 1973, which now takes place in June or July on the lawns of Charlton House in South London, having run for over 300 years before being closed down due to general licentiousness in 1874. Likewise, Stourbridge Fair, mentioned before, and one of four fairs held in Cambridge (and at one point said to be the largest fair in Europe), was revived in 2003 after closing down seventy years earlier following a period of steady decline, as was Mitcham Fair.

While steam and nostalgia may have helped rescue the smaller travelling fair, scale became increasingly important for the more established charter fairs, and through the 1980s and '90s showmen increasingly abandoned their ex-Army vehicles and adopted big, modern, articulated lorries to transport larger and larger rides, with the expansion of the motorway network making it easier to get from place to place. With the public getting used to ever more elaborate rides such as looping or inverted roller coasters, giant observational wheels, log flumes and sky flyers, it was perhaps inevitable that the potential for permanent fairs – once epitomised by the seaside parks such as Belle Vue in Manchester and the Kursaal in Southend, which by the end of the 1970s had either closed or were in terminal decline – would re-enter the public consciousness.

To the fanfare of much publicity, the installation of a triple corkscrew ride in 1980 heralded the arrival of the permanent theme park at Alton Towers in Staffordshire. Thorpe Park in Surrey had opened as an educational park the year before, but it rapidly made large white-knuckle rides its hallmark in the wake of Alton Towers. Others followed, including Drayton Manor, also in Staffordshire, and Chessington World of Adventures, which opened in 1987 on the site of the old Chessington Zoo.

The opening of the Triple Corkscrew at Alton Towers heralded a new era for theme parks.

With growing prosperity, there was room for a spectrum of fairs, from small town private businesses, through to steam fairs, larger charter fairs and established theme parks. Some showmen also branched out into designing and building rides during this time. Towards the end of the millennium, fairs were obliged to come into line with the modern requirement to meet rules and regulations. Following the disaster at Battersea, a new testing regime came into force on rides, with stresses having to be calculated and rigorous inspections becoming the norm. At the same time, self-imposed rules among the show fraternity discouraged speculative travelling to different fairs, with 'grounds' or spots at a fair being allocated by common agreement to particular showmen or their families. This, along with the rising cost of fuel, encouraged the development of regional operators, leaving the national circuit only really viable for those with large rides capable of generating good trade. A combination of an increasingly regulated society and sheer economic reality was coming together to force the fair to respond once again to forces beyond its control.

8

A Breed Apart

As this book has shown, showmen and their families have always been, and always will be, at the heart of the travelling fair; but who are they, and what's it like to live the showman's way of life?

Most of the showmen in England and Scotland can trace their family history within the fairground industry back for many generations – in some cases for hundreds of years. Given their transient life, and the sense that their chosen lifestyle somehow sets them apart from the punters they earn their living from, it's probably no surprise to learn that these families tend to be tight-knit, with skills being passed down from father to son or daughter.

Equally, the fact that they all earn their living in the same way, that they face the same challenges year in, year out, and are constantly in each other's company means that it is similarly unsurprising that these families have formed a community that tends to look after each other, and even has its own shared language. Apart from a few outsiders involved in the business and enthusiasts, show people tend to socialise among themselves in a way that 'flatties' or 'joskins', as showmen call people who have never lived a travelling life, may find difficult to comprehend.

Meticulous about cleanliness, it is a recent development that travelling people would have a sink and toilet inside their living wagons, as they tended to prefer keeping the necessities of keeping clean apart from day-to-day living. Until relatively recently, all showmen would have a built-up toilet that stood near their wagon for their exclusive use. There were no public toilets on a ground or site (although it is now a requirement), so staff had to locate the nearest public facilities or hide behind a hedge.

More often than not, showmen marry the daughters of show folk, even to the extent of ride owners going with ride owners and side stuff lessees marrying within their group of friends. This results in some very useful alliances of families regarding rights and privileges at big fairs. Within these families, bonds of trust form – something that is particularly important when dealing with potentially dangerous machinery and, until recently, often quite significant amounts of cash.

The way of life for show people is governed by building up, opening, pulling down and moving to the next gaff, ground or site, week after week, month after month and year after year. The season traditionally starts with King's Lynn Mart on 14 February, or Leeds Valentines Fair, which is followed by the Easter Fairs and Kirkcaldy Links Fair in Scotland. Although showmen spend most of their time on the road, they also tend to have their own 'yards', or bases, and following Easter this is where they will retreat to, perhaps to conduct some running repairs or to engage in some private business at small local fairs.

The May bank holidays mark the next phase of the season, with the main event in June being the Hoppings Fair on Newcastle Town Moor. Throughout the summer, showmen will work to keep busy with town shows, race meetings, steam rallies, country shows, music festivals, car shows and local funfairs. Surprisingly, the summer is not the most lucrative period for showmen, with most traditional charter fairs taking place on either side of these months. It is generally a case of keeping busy during July and most of August, while using the money made at the start of the season to tide things over.

When the children are on holiday in August, a number of showmen will head to the coast with their rides until the back end run – the part of the season that can make or break a year. This is when things get very busy, with the St Giles Fair in Oxford, as well as Bridgwater, Nottingham, Hull, and all the mop fairs, such as Stratford, all coming one after the other, and the end of the season now being marked by bonfire fairs. These fairs involve a lot of hard work, as two or three are attended in a week, which necessitates building up and pulling down all night and all day. The fair is usually only open for a few hours before the bonfire is lit and then for an hour or two after the fireworks. Money can be taken in November if the weather is kind but if it starts to 'parnee' (the showmen's

Winter Wonderlands, such as the one in Hyde Park, London, have stretched the season.

word for rain) then the punters tend to rush off home, leaving the showmen with the prospect of pulling down and moving on with little reward for their efforts. Like farmers, showmen show an interest in the weather forecast that goes far beyond what sort of coat to take, as a bad weekend can have a disproportionate impact on takings while outgoings remain constant.

In December, the small juvenile rides are taken to Christmas lights switch-on evenings, and these have also become increasingly popular with Christmas parties, with large rides like Dodgems and Gallopers being hired out for corporate office parties. Christmas fairs in large town centres have also grown in popularity in recent years, including the Winter Wonderland held in Hyde Park, London, and those inside exhibition centres, where large rides from the continent compete for business with UK equipment. These can include funhouses and ghost houses three times the size of their UK equivalent with ornate fronts, as well as large looping roller coasters.

After Christmas, time is spent on the maintenance of equipment, in building new rides, as well as in servicing and getting the lorries and trailers plated and tested. Another important job usually carried out at this time of year is engaging the services of an ADIPS (Amusement Device Inspection Procedures Scheme) inspection body (IB) tester to inspect and issue a DOC (Declaration of Operational Compliance) for the coming year. This scheme was set up in conjunction with the Health and Safety Executive following the Roberts Report into Fairground Safety, which came out on 2 August 2001 following a number of fatalities on amusement rides. There is now an HSE Code of Safe Practice at Fairs (HSG 175), which all operators must adhere to.

The new year can be another busy time of year, with weddings between show folk usually taking place in the winter months. Like funerals and christenings, they are well attended by show people from far and wide, and are always reported in the showman's weekly paper *World's Fair* so that everyone can see who did and didn't attend. As mentioned previously, fairground folk are a very proud and close-knit community. The children are acclimatised to life on the gaff from birth, immediately after which they spend their time in a Silver Cross pram by the side of a joint or ride, being looked after by parents or grandparents.

When they get a bit older, all their playmates are from the fair, with new friends having to be made at each new place, and as teenagers they soon find themselves looking after a joint or hoopla. A few show families send the children off to boarding school, but this is not very popular with the children as they often have trouble fitting in and tend to miss their travelling way of life, which gets into the bloodstream. At the end of January or the beginning of February, many families meet up in Tenerife to enjoy a week or two on holiday with friends and family before pulling out for the start of the season, and the cycle begins again.

By tradition, when the eldest son marries he takes over running a family ride or show, opening at fairs where the rights and privileges have belonged to that family for generations. Good positions at major fairs for rides and joints are invaluable to show families when it comes to convincing a bank manager to lend them as much as £500,000 to buy a new ride, as the land belongs to the council or landowner, so the bank needs to be assured that a family has the right places to earn the money needed to repay the loan. The days of showmen financing new rides from cash, or through informal 'arrangements'

Rides get ever more sensational, such as this Meteorite and Danter's Air ride at St Giles, Oxford...

...and this Freakout at Thame Fair.

A group of Silver Cross prams – the pram of choice amongst show families.

with the manufacturer, such as forwarding notes and coins in barrels as stage payments, as happened in Savage's day, are now firmly in the past.

Although pulling back into the yard is looked forward to at the end of the season, and it is good to catch up with winter repairs, the first fairs of the season are eagerly awaited once the nights start drawing out to start taking money again, as there is not much left in the bank by the time the vehicles are taxed, the insurance is paid and the tanks are filled with fuel. A typical week during the season would start by pulling the loads on Monday or Tuesday morning, which might mean doubling back once or twice with a lorry to collect another ride or living trailer. Once the ground has been marked out by the lessee, the living trailers have been set up on one side of the fair and the staff trailers have been parked up with the lorries on the other side, building up can start.

These days, a modern trailer-mounted ride or show does not require the manpower the old build-up-from-the-ground rides took, when every showman needed a staff of three or four people (who were known as 'gaff lads', 'gaff girls', 'chaps', or just 'the men'). These were a breed apart, usually with a gold ring on one ear and tattoos, possibly saying GAFF across the knuckles on their right hand and LAD across the left, or other identifiers such as SKID, ARK, DODGEM or WALTZER on their arms.

The gaff lads would also be notorious for having a different 'mossy', or girl, waiting for them in every town. Despite these benefits, it is quite hard to find good staff willing to travel with the fair today, which is not surprising when you can be better off on the dole!

Above: Three generations of the Noyce showman's family inspect the newly carved rounding boards for their set of Gallopers.

Right: A new Skyflyer under construction in Tommy Matthews' winter quarters.

If there was any trouble the gaff lads would always stick together and help each other out. Should the 'gavvers', or police, come on a ground looking for 'chordy', or stolen goods, no one in the show fraternity would have even thought of grassing on a fellow traveller. This old way of life was portrayed in the 1973 film *That'll Be The Day* starring David Essex as a fairground Lothario in the 1950s/60s, with Ringo Starr in a supporting role, along with Freddie Beadle's Ark, or Whip. Engage an old gaff lad in conversation and most will agree these were the best years of their life and they wished they'd never settled down to be a flattie, and indeed many continue to help out as casuals for a pull down.

Having had breakfast, work starts about 9 a.m. the next day, and building up continues until everything is ready to open. The day before opening is often spent washing the mud from the previous place off the rides and transport, and even polishing the showman's living wagon, emptying the toilets and filling up water tanks. Thursday is usually opening night, which is sometimes advertised as half-price night. Friday night used to be a good night as most workers got their wage packets that day, but these days most people receive a monthly salary paid directly into the bank. Therefore, most of today's fairgrounds have to have a kiosk where punters can buy tokens (using a credit card) to spend on the ground. Saturday and Sunday are family days if the weather is good. As soon as the last ride is over and the fair closes, pulling down commences. Very often this continues all through the night whatever the weather, especially if there is a rush to get to the next gaff, after which the cycle starts all over again.

Proudly independent, showmen and their families are one of the few truly nomadic groups left in a society that generally places great value on home ownership. Along with their shared traditions and workplace, this tends to reinforce the sense that they are a breed apart,

Left: Mark, complete with his hi-vis, has been a gaff lad for over thirty years.

Right: Building up, whatever the weather.

Building up. Again, note the hi-vis jackets.

encouraging the sort of resilience and flexibility that has continually cropped up in telling the story of the fair. Being on the move, it's difficult to form close friendships outside the showmen's circle, and on arriving at a new gaff they may be viewed with an air of suspicion by existing traders who fear a loss of business, upheaval and maybe traffic chaos. Heightened sensibility towards the possible attitudes of different authorities and the police, with show folk sometimes being convenient scapegoats for any trouble, can add to this tension.

Showmen have each other though, and in the end this bond is the strongest. They are part of a wider community, and a key voice for that community has been the Showmen's Guild of Great Britain. The role the Guild has played in the modern history of the fair has already been mentioned a number of times in this narrative, and any person involved in the amusement industry in the UK, whether or not they are a member of the Guild, will find his or her business is influenced and affected by the Showmen's Guild of Great Britain and its members.

As early as 1911, when the president was the renowned showman Patrick Collins (also Mayor and briefly MP for Walsall), the Showmen's Guild lodged petitions in its own name, and in 1917 it became a registered trade union, which meant it could implement a set of rules for its members, especially regarding safety. Many leading showmen have been President of the Guild, with the post held today by J. C. Culine MBE, and the role is virtually a full-time job these days. The Guild is organised into ten sections: London and Home Counties (which is the largest section), Western, South Wales, Eastern Counties, Notts and Derby, Northern, Lancashire, Yorkshire, Midland and Scottish sections. The Guild is now a trade association and has a central office in Staines, Middlesex.

9

Present and Future

If this history has told us anything, it is that the continuing survival of the travelling fair is dependent upon being in tune with, and responding to, changing times and circumstances. With a new millennium, and an almost overwhelming range of entertainment options (many of which seem to encourage solitary rather than social engagement), this challenge remains as great as ever. Increasing regulation, economic uncertainty, changes in technology, an ever more diverse society and the need for constant innovation – none of these are particularly new; but the pace and impact of change seems to be accelerating at such a rate that it's difficult to predict the future for the fair with any certainty.

What we do know is that showmen have proven to be remarkably adept at responding to change in the past, and there is no reason that they won't rise to meet these new challenges in the future. In fact, there is plenty of evidence to say that they already are. One example is the shift away from cash being taken directly from the punter's own hand in favour of token or wristband systems. As well as providing greater security, this can be seen as a response to the move towards an increasingly cashless economy, especially among the fair's core market of the young, and it has had a significant impact. Traditionally reluctant to discuss money outside the family circle, showmen have had to get used to being more open and to adopt the practices of more traditional businesses, such as registering for VAT and paying via PAYE, rather than cash-in-hand.

At the same time, in a response to an increasingly safety conscious, and indeed litigious, society, CCTV is now common practice on rides in order to provide evidence should an accident occur (a side effect of which is that there are now few hiding places for any side deals!) Whereas the public might once have been happy to snack on hot dogs, toffee apples and candy floss, they are now offered gourmet coffee, baguettes and curries. Where once a plaster ornament or a piece of carnival glass might once have sufficed as a prize, these days a cuddly toy or piece of merchandise from the summer's blockbuster movie is more likely. That said, although live goldfish in a bag as prizes may have lost their popularity (although some showmen still offer them in bowls, along with some fish food), bow and arrow sets still seem to retain their fascination for small boys.

Equally, while most showmen still need to be accomplished mechanics to ensure both the smooth running of their rides as well as their vehicles, most have had to adapt to

Cash is fast becoming a thing of the past.

both of these being controlled more by computer than by dials and levers, and they have adapted well. On a more basic, but still significant, technological level, showmen have also learned to embrace LEDs rather than traditional lightbulbs to light their shows at night, which saves on electricity consumption, but offers a different type of ambiance. Electronics have also enabled even the largest ride to be built up almost at the touch of a button; where it might once have taken four men to build a set of Gallopers up over a day, the same task can now be accomplished by two men in half a day.

Showmen have also responded well to changing demand. The modern public seems to crave fresh, new experiences, and showmen have proved skilled at meeting these demands by supplying rides such as Dodgems and Gallopers at events like weddings, corporate events, May Balls, music festivals, and in fact most places where significant numbers of people gather together, in an echo of the fair's roots in markets. Events such as the British Grand Prix or an awards show now seem to need to offer more than just their primary purpose to satisfy the paying public, and showmen have proved willing to provide that extra thrill, or an opportunity to revel in nostalgia. These bookings have also helped to smooth out cash flow, with most showmen now able to generate income most of the year round, with Halloween Ghost Trains and Christmas Wonderlands also offering good opportunities to supplement earnings from the traditional charter fairs.

Fairground fare, old and new.

Many fairs have been around for hundreds of years.

The demands of modern society mean that fairs have to operate within a safe environment, and as a consequence some of the 'edge' of the old fairground has inevitably been rubbed off. Greasy, dirty overalls are no longer acceptable, especially if the customers are dressed in ball gowns and morning suits, with many ride attendants now wearing a corporate uniform or hi-vis jacket. In another expression of what society deems as acceptable, shows featuring counting pigs or 'freaks' are no longer seen as appropriate for public entertainment.

Being able to make money has always been important, but these days the line between profit and loss is being stretched increasingly thin, with local authorities demanding more in rent and stipulating levels of security, ground bonds, temporary toilets and first aiders, which all add to expenses. Throw in the rising costs for advertising, fuel for generating electricity and for road vehicles, insurance and general maintenance costs, all at a time when the average wages of the paying public have remained static, and the result is that only the fittest survive. Finally, there are the perennial concerns of demand on the day and uncertain weather, which affect everyone. Taken together, today's reality is that private businesses or small fairs are barely viable.

As if changing society, increasing regulation and burgeoning costs weren't enough, competition for the public's pound doesn't look like it is going away. Theme parks in particular seem to show no sign of losing their appeal, with plans for a new £2 billion Disneyland-style theme park twice the size of the 2012 Olympic Park due to start construction in 2018/19 near Ebbsfleet, in Kent, featuring attractions licensed from Paramount Pictures, the BBC and Aardman Studios. This proposed park gives a glimpse into the potential future of these large attractions, with the park – in line with other large developments abroad – offering a variety of entertainments including cinemas, a water park and hotels, therefore increasing both its appeal, and its risk.

Meanwhile, attraction-only based theme parks, such as those introduced in the 1980s, have shown their vulnerability to accidents, with Alton Towers suffering a downfall in visitor numbers following a crash on its Smiler roller coaster in 2015, which seriously injured four customers, and the unfortunate death of a young girl in an accident on the Splash Canyon attraction at Drayton Manor in 2017.

As if all this wasn't enough, the Showmen's Guild, which has done so much to keep the fair alive and to monitor standards, itself became the target of an accusation of restrictive practices from the Competitions & Markets Authority (CMA) in late December 2016. In effect, the CMA issued a set of objections to the Guild, stating that some of its practices protect Guild members and reduce competition, making it hard for non-Guild members to join or establish fairs, thereby breaching competition law.

This accusation was described as 'the greatest challenge to showmen since the formation of the Guild' by the showmen's paper *World's Fair*, prompting a rigorous defence of its practices by the Guild. The industry clearly faced a dilemma. Over time, the rules provided by the Guild have provided a framework to allow showmen to operate and meet the various challenges put before them. To have those rules characterised as uncompetitive put the very purpose and existence of the Guild at risk, and losing it, and its advocacy for the fair, would deliver a massive blow to traditional showmen.

One thing showmen can't control is the weather!

Following much discussion, the Showman's Guild offered to amend its rules in August 2017, with key points being:

- Making it easier to join the Guild, thereby making it easier for previous non-members to take ground at fairs run by non-members and for non-members to attend fairs run by the Guild,
- Making it easier for landowners to replace underperforming showmen with those able to offer a better service,
- Reducing restrictions on how close fairs can operate, bringing it down to 1 mile, against the previous limit of 2 miles,
- Allowing members to attend events and festivals with all types of rides,
- Making the Guild's rulebook more transparent by making it available online.

At the time of writing, the CMA was inclined to accept these proposals and drop its investigation, and had invited members of the public to comment on the Guild's proposals.

Above: The freak show has proved to be remarkably resilient.

Below: Inflatables prove popular with younger children.

Above: Some things never change, such as the perennial Hook-a-Duck, even if these days a prize has to be offered every time.

Below: Perhaps appealing to base instincts?

These days, goldfish won at the fair need to be taken home in RSPCA-approved containers rather than plastic bags.

It is impossible to know exactly what the future holds for the fair, and whether it will continue to be operated by traditional showmen, by entertainment conglomerates or by individuals trying their luck. As the previous chapter has shown, however, being a showman is a way of life, not just another business. It is influenced, but not ruled by, the economics that may determine the fate of rival attractions or large commercial entertainment suppliers. So long as it is worth their while, traditional showmen will continue to invest their time and money in rides and equipment just to be on the road.

They are also invested personally in their business, and customers can sense the difference between being enticed into parting with their cash by an experienced showman whose livelihood, and that of his family, depends on their ability to enthral and entertain you, against being served by a disinterested employee absorbed in their mobile phone. For the showman, even if the takings sometimes only just cover their expenses, taking money is better than simply pulling back into the yard, but that remains a big 'if'.

What we do know is that the fair has always been part of our culture, and in order to survive it has shown a remarkable ability through the centuries to change with the times.

A set of Gondolas at Dingles Fairground Heritage Centre in Devon.

In doing so it has rooted itself deep in our national consciousness to the extent that there are centres dedicated to recording and preserving its special place in our history, such as Dingles Fairground Heritage Centre in Devon, the Vintage Fairground at Folly Farm in Wales (which offers 'all the thrills of yesteryear'), and the National Fairground and Circus Archive at the University of Sheffield. The challenge now is to prevent these from becoming repositories for a life that has passed, rather than examples of a still-living story.

For now, the fairground industry still offers over 8,000 pieces of amusement equipment and generates around £100 million worth of income a year. It would be foolish to underestimate the challenges that lie ahead, however. As we have seen, keeping the fair alive for the generations to come is becoming an ever-increasing challenge. That said, the fair has deep roots in our psyche and showmen have demonstrated resilience in the past. It has successfully resisted legal challenges and predictions of its demise before, and it is to be hoped that the qualities that have seen it through before are enough to allow it to continue to thrive in the future.

The public have a role to play in keeping the fairground going for future generations too. Remember, if you don't visit your local fair, don't be surprised if next time it isn't there.

Polling down.

The Fair Calendar

Today, the main fairs of England are as follows:

February

Downham Market Fair
King's Lynn Mart opens 14 February, St Valentine's Day
Lichfield Fair
Stalybridge Fair

March

Blackheath Easter Fair
Hampstead Heath, London
Hampton Court Easter Fair
Lichfield Shrovetide Fair
Pontardawe Fair
Southampton Common Easter Fair

April

Clapham Common Fair
Grantham Mid Lent Fair
Kirkcaldy Links Market
Scunthorpe Fair
Stamford Mid Lent Fair

May

Beaconsfield Fair
Boston May Fair, opening the first Wednesday in May
Brighton on the Level Fair
Broadway Wake Fair
Chipping Campden Scuttlebrook Wake Fair
Coventry Pot Fair
Crystal Palace May Fair
Ealing Common Fair
Godstone Green
Knutsford Royal May Day Fair
Northampton May Fair
Pinkneys Green Steam Fair
Pinner Street Fair
Stow-on-the-Wold Street Fair

June

Bristol Midsummer Fair
Bromyard Gala
Cambridge Midsummer Fair
Coventry Carnival
Epsom Derby Fair
Newcastle Town Moor Festival
Peterborough Cherry Fair
Towcester Fair

July

Brockwell Park Brixton
Cheltenham Festival Fair
Chester-le-Street Fair
Dartmouth Regatta
Haywards Heath Fair
Henley Regatta
Kettering Feast
Poole Regatta
Praze Fair
Spennymoor Gala
Warrington Walking Day Fair

August

Babbacombe Regatta
Bank Holiday Monday fairs at Blackheath, Wanstead, Hampstead Heath
Great Dorset Steam Fair
Lea Gap Fair
Long Buckby Feast
Lutterworth Feast
Malvern Link Fair
Mitcham Fair
Southend Carnival

September

Annesley Miners Gala
Ashby-de-la-Zouch Statute Fair
Barnet Fair
Barnstable (Barum) Fair
Birmingham Onion Fair
Bridgwater St Matthews Fair
Findon Sheep Fair
Glastonbury Tor Fair
Helston Harvest Fair
Neath Great Fair
Newton Abbott Cheese and Onion Fair
Scarborough Fair
Summercourt Fair
St Giles Fair, Oxford
Thame Street Fair
Witney Feast, Oxon

October

Abingdon Michaelmas Fair
Banbury Michaelmas Fair
Chichester Sloe Fair
Daventry Mops
Ely Fair
Faversham Fair
Hull Pleasure Fair
Ilkeston Charter Fair
Newbury Michaelmas Fair

Nottingham Goose Fair
Stratford-upon-Avon Mop
Peterborough Bridge Fair
Tavistock Goose Fair
Tewkesbury Mop Fair
Woodstock Street Fair

November

Belper Fair
Bonfire Fairs
Deddington Market Place Fair
Loughborough Charter Fair
Petworth Street Fair

December

Christmas Fairs
Kelvin Hall Glasgow
Winter Wonderland in Hyde Park London and Manchester

Suggested Further Reading

The following books have been useful in compiling this book and offer further reading for those wishing to delve deeper into the world of the funfair:

Bleackley, H. W., *The Hangmen of England* (E. P. Publishing, 1976)

Bonser, K. J., *The Drovers* (Country Book Club, 1972)

Braithwaite, D., *Fairground Architecture* (F. A. Praeger, 1968)

Brown, F., *Fairfield Folk: A History of the British Fairground and Its People* (Malvern Publishing Co. Ltd, 1968)

Dallas, D., *The Travelling People* (Macmillan, 1971)

Disher, M. W., *Fairs Circuses & Music Halls* (William Collins, 1942)

Kerr Cameron, D., *The English Fair* (Sutton Publishing, 1998)

Lukens, J., *The Sanger Story* (Hodder & Stoughton, 1956)

Muncey, R. W., *Our Old English Fairs* (Sheldon Press, 1906)

Roope, F. C., *Come to the Fair* (Showmen's Guild, 1961)

Sanger, G., *Seventy Years A Showman* (J. M. Dent, 1927)

Starsmore, Ian, *English Fairs* (Thames & Hudson, 1975)

Townsend, K., *Fairgrounds at War 1939–1945* (K. Townsend, 2010)

Toulmin, V., Downie, G., Campbell, J. and Trowell, I., *Heart of England Fairs* (The History Press, 2000)

Williams, N., *Midland Fairground Families* (Uralia Press, 1996)